Walter Chalmers Smith

# Kildrostan

A Dramatic Poem

Walter Chalmers Smith

**Kildrostan**
*A Dramatic Poem*

ISBN/EAN: 9783744696333

Printed in Europe, USA, Canada, Australia, Japan

Cover: Foto ©Thomas Meinert / pixelio.de

More available books at **www.hansebooks.com**

# KILDROSTAN

*A DRAMATIC POEM*

BY

WALTER C. SMITH

𝔊lasgow

JAMES MACLEHOSE AND SONS

PUBLISHERS TO THE UNIVERSITY

1884

# Dramatis Personæ.

SIR DIARMID MACALPINE, - - *Highland Chief.*

TREMAIN, - - - - - *A Modern Poet.*

DR. LORNE, - - - - *Uncle to Ina.*

BENNETT, - - - - *Lawyer.*

DUFFUS, - - - - - *Factor.*

KENNETH, - - - - *A Poor Student.*

CHUNDRA, - - - - *Servant to Dr. Lorne.*

MINISTERS, "MEN," CROFTERS, ETC.


LADY MACALPINE, - - - *Mother of Sir Diarmid.*

INA LORNE, - - - - *Minister's Daughter.*

DORIS CATTANACH, - - *A Highland Proprietress.*

MAIRI CATTANACH, - - *Her Cousin.*

MORAG, - - - - - *Ina's Old Nurse.*

MRS. SLIT, - - - - *Post-mistress.*

FISHERWOMEN, ETC.


## Chorus.

# KILDROSTAN.

## ACT FIRST.—SCENE FIRST.

### Chorus.

Poor fishers on the wild west shore
  Where slow mists trail along the hills,
And from the mist comes evermore
  The sound of rushing brooks and rills,
Are plodding, grave, with lingering feet,
  About the high hot noon of day,
Along the circle of the street
  That straggles round the circling bay.

Why are the long-oared boats afloat?
  Why tolls the bell from the steepled kirk?
It is not the hour to launch the boat,
  And it is not the Sabbath of rest from work;
And why are they all in best array,
As it were for some high holiday?

A

'Neath crags and hills the long loch winds,
　Through rocky isles where sea-birds flock;
Along the slopes the grey birch finds
　Frail footing on the slaty rock;
On every ledge there grows a pine,
　With roots that cling as the branches toss,
And the oaks along the low sea-line
　Are greenly feathered with fern and moss.
Behind the cliffs are mountains steep
　By foaming torrents scored and scarred,
And up their gullies the alders creep,
　But the peaks are ragged and jagged and barred:
Cloud-capped often their stormy tops,
　While ridge and corrie and crag are bare,
Or a girdle of mist will ring the slopes,
　While the heights rise clear in the upper air.

A desolate land of fern and moss,
　Of brackened braes and craggy hills,
And shores where fickle waters toss,
　And birch-and-hazel-fringéd rills
And foaming cataracts like snow
　That in the gorges leap and run,
And rocks, ice-polished long ago,
　That gleam like waters in the sun,
And rainbows arching high in heaven

And down in still lochs doubly bowed,
While broken prismic lights are woven
  On the thin veils of wavering cloud,
And gorgeous sunsets that enfold
  The mountains with a purple robe,
And dash the crimson and the gold
  In billowy spray about the globe:
A land of wayside cairns—the place
  Of resting for the biers of death—
And tokens of a fading race,
  And relics of forgotten faith—
Legend and rhyme and mystic rite,
  The worship of a God unknown,
Stealthily done at dead of night
  By sacred well or standing stone.
O marvel not they love the land
  Who watch its changeful hills and skies,
For in its desolation grand
  A charm of 'wildering beauty lies.


A meagre life they have, and still—
  Not stiller almost is the grave—
Those villagers beneath the hill
  That looks down on the encircling wave;
Rude are the huts of stone and turf
  That straggle round the circling street,

The thatched roofs soaked with rain or surf,
 And blackened with the smoking. peat.
No ploughshare tears the scanty soil,
 Enough for them are spade and hoe;
'Tis on the waters that they toil,
 And in the seas their harvests grow.
The moors are for the hare and grouse,
 The corries for the antlered stag,   .
But shaggy big-horned cattle browse
 On the fringe of bracken and rush and flag.
And now and then comes like a dream
 A white-sailed yacht into the bay,
And now and then the snort of steam
 Sounds from the headland far away;
But never shows the world's proud strife,
 Its strain of power, and rush of thought:
Time counts for nothing in their life,
 But comes and goes, and changes nought.
Yet men have grown there, true and brave,
 Bronzed with weather, and horny of hand,
Who wrestled with the problems grave
 That at the porch of Wisdom stand;
And you shall find in low, thatched cot,
 Round-angled, and with smoke begrimed,
Love that can sweeten every lot,
 And Faith that hath all fates sublimed.

But why are the long-oared boats afloat?
  Why tolls the bell from the steepled kirk?
It is not the hour to launch the boat,
  And it is not the Sabbath of rest from work;
And why are the children sad and grave,
With no ripple of mirth by the rippling wave?
And whither away do the strong men walk,
While the women gather in groups and talk?

SCENE—*Village Street of Kinloch-Thorar.  Group of Women at the Post Office Door.*

*First Fisherwoman.*—Ochone! but this iss a sad day on Loch Thorar, Mrs. Slit.

*Mrs. Slit.*—You may say that, 'Lizbeth, and in Glen Shelloch too, and Glen Turret, which iss more.

*First Fisherwoman.*—He wass a good man, and a faithful minister.  He wass not a dumb dog that will be gnawing the bones, and will not bark when he should.

*Mrs. Slit.*—Och, yes! he wass all that, though he might not preach like Black Rory of Skye, or big John of Strathnaver.  But he would not be passing my shop door without getting pickles of snuff for the old men, and sweeties too for the greeting bairns.  Yes, yes! it will not be the same shop now that he does not come here any more.

*Second Fisherwoman.*—But what iss this, Mrs. Slit? She will not be for burying him in the kirkyard, but in Isle-Monach, where my Donald would be seeing their ghosts at Yule and Pasch.

*Mrs. Slit.*—It iss your Donald that would be having the whisky, then. For they will be quiet men, the monks, when they are living, and they will not be frisky now that they are in their graves.

*Second Fisherwoman.*—But they are in Purgatory, whatever; and our minister had no faith in Purgatory or organs or saints or good works. Why would she be for burying him among them? Iss it papist she will be turning?

*First Fisherwoman.*—Or Pagan, Mrs. Slit? For our May wass saying she would read more about heathen gods and goddesses than about Abraham or Moses; and May wass maid in the manse till Candlemas last.

*Mrs. Slit.*—May will not know what young ladies have to know. And which iss more, she might do better than to be talking about her betters. As for Purgatory, it iss not any more, since the laird's great grandfather forbade it, or it will only be for the poor cottars at Glen Chroan. And whether or no, our minister will have nothing to do with it, you may be sure. But it iss true

Miss Ina never wass just like other maids. But her heart iss good, whatever, yes! and which iss more, it iss soft and warm as a linnet's nest, and sweeter as the bog-myrtle.

*Third Fisherwoman.*—Och yes! it will be warm and sweet, but not good, Mrs. Slit. None of our hearts iss good, as he would often say, who will never say it any more. But many a time, when the lads wass out fishing, it iss Miss Ina that would hail them from her bit boatie, and she would have the kind word for each of them; yes! and she would call at our doors too on her way home, and tell us about Dugald or Donald or Alisthair and the herrings. Och yes! she hass the kind heart, whatever, and it will be a sorry one this day.

*First Fisherwoman.*—Yes! she hass the kind heart, Miss Ina; and if she would have the making of the law, it would be the better for us, though it iss true she iss for making the men carry the peats, and wade out to the boats too, which it would be a shame for women to see.

*Second Fisherwoman.*—But whose boat will she be having, now? For it iss a rhyme I heard long ago—

> Coffined corpse in fisher's boat;
> Make ready a shroud when it's next afloat.

*Mrs. Slit.*—The de'il an ye were in your shroud, woman, to speak of such a thing ! Do you know that it iss Sir Diarmid himself that will bring his gig and his gillies and his piper too, all in the brave tartan, with plaid and sporran, as if the minister would be a chief, for he was not more than third cousin to the laird's grandfather. And it iss the chief that you would be singing your carline rhymes about, and making a shroud for him too !

*Second Fisherwoman.*—But he iss not a fisher.

*Mrs. Slit.*—He will fish more than your Donald, whatever : for when he iss in the humour, the loch iss never in trim; and when the loch iss in the humour, he hass no inclination. But it iss not for you, woman, to be speaking of the laird and a shroud in one breath, and him a brave young gentleman, and which iss more, just growing the beautiful beard too. Yes !

*First Fisherwoman.*—But why will she be for burying him among the monks, when there iss a Christian kirkyard at her door, Mrs. Slit ?

*Mrs. Slit.*—Who hass a better right to lie there? For he comes of the old stock that built the Abbey Kirk; and all their graves are there, and there iss nobody else but chiefs and monks and ministers and superior persons, which iss proper. There has not been a burial there since old Sir Kenneth's, the day of the great storm, when half our boats were wrecked, and the poor lads were bobbing about the loch, like pellocks in a gale of wind.

*Third Fisherwoman.*—Ochone! yes; and it is myself will mind it, if I am spared to my dying day. My Alisthair, that wass to be married just the week after, drifted ashore among the tangles before his Mysie's door, and she will never be herself again since that fery hour. And it wass Miss Ina that would have the bodies carried to the kirk, and the funeral there; for they will preach to us, said she, better than the minister, or an angel from heaven.

*First Fisherwoman.*—Sure, and she wass right there, for there would not be a profane swearer or a Sabbath-breaker in the parish for six months after, though the whisky wass wanted for the sore heart sometimes, maybe.

*Mrs. Slit.*—Yes! it wass a great sermon, the lads lying in a row, and just the day before they had talked to us, and which iss more, they had laughed with us; and now they looked at us, and would not know us any more. Och yes! it wass a great sermon, and it wass God himself that preached it. But there, now; they are leaving the manse.

It iss our own lads that will be carrying the coffin with its white wreaths and ferns.   Och! and Sir Diarmid and Miss Ina make the handsome pair, like the brown pine and the bonnie birch tree.   She iss liker him than that Doris, with her mouth that iss always smiling, and her eyes that never do.

*First Fisherwoman.*—But they will be saying he must marry Doris, whatever.

*Mrs. Slit.*—Maybe yes, maybe no.   It iss not every fish you hook that comes to the creel; and the stag iss not on the spit because Donald has loaded his gun.   And that will be her uncle, the Doctor, that wass the ne'er-do-well, and nearly broke his brother's heart, and which is more, emptied his purse too.   But he iss come home now, they say, as rich as the English lord at Loch Eylert.   Sure they will rest the coffin somewhere or his cairn, and for the drop whisky.   There and now Eachan Macrimmon is playing a coronach as it were for a chief.   "Peace to his soul, and a stone to his cairn."

### CHORUS.

Slowly the muffled oars dip in the tide,
Slowly the silent boats shadow-like glide
Past the grey, steepled kirk, past the low manse,

Now in the ripples that glimmer and glance
Where the sun flashes, and now in the shade
The birch-feathered rocks and the great hills have
    made ;
Slowly and silently onward they pass
Over the calm spaces shining like glass,
While wild wailing strains of the coronach swell,
And fall with the breeze and the slow-tolling bell.
Long, low and dark is the first of the train,
With six bending oars keeping time to the strain ;
In it a coffin, and by it a maiden
Who to the moaning sea moans sorrow-laden,
As they drop down to the dim abbey pile
Lying half-hid in a cleft of the isle,
Ruined and roofless, 'mid tangle of trees
That dip their low boughs in the wave, but the
    breeze
Rustles their higher leaves over a tower
Green with massed ivy, and crown'd with wall-flower.
There, with his forefathers, peaceful to sleep
By the white surf of the unresting deep,
Where once the Culdee monk toiled, prayed, and
    died,
Where once the galleys oared out in their pride,
Where still the clansmen their high chiefs bewail,
Silent they laid the good priest of the Gael.

No cross was reared above his head,
No requiem was sung or said,
No hope was spoken of the just
In glory rising from the dust:
In silent awe they did their part,
Yet the good hope was in every heart.


## ACT FIRST.—SCENE SECOND.

### CHORUS.

A little wiry man, with grizzled hair,
And withered face that wrinkled was and bare,
And clear keen eyes that had no look of care,
    Sat with a maid
All robed in black, herself a lily white,
Beautiful as the moon in starless night
Whose silent depths alternate wondrous light
    And mystic shade.

Blunt in his speech, a careless nature his,
A wanderer driven by restless impulses,
Nor many years had toned his heedlessness,
    Nor loss nor gain:
And nothing awed him that the world reveres,

Yet was he awed before a maiden's tears,
And stumbled in his talk with doubts and fears
    Of giving pain.

He would be gentle, if he but knew how,
And helpful, if his gold could help her now,
But wist not of the deeper life, I trow,
    Patient and meek;
And woman's ways had long been strange to him,
And eyes, unused to weeping, now grew dim
Seeing her eyes in shining waters swim,
    And tear-stained cheek.


SCENE—*The Manse Parlour.*  INA *and* DR. LORNE *searching books and papers.*

### Dr. Lorne.

This clean bewilders me: it is like being
Lost in a mist, and wandering round 'and round,
To end where you began, only more puzzled,
Weary and hopeless.  What can he have done
With it, I wonder.

### Ina.

    Uncle, what is wrong?

### Dr. Lorne.

Oh ! nothing's wrong of course.  It's only I
Am growing old and stupid, I suppose.
I'm puzzled, that is all.

#### Ina.

                  But what about?
And can I help you?   Yet if it is dark
To you, I fear that my poor head to-day
Can bring but little light.

#### Dr. Lorne.

                  O never mind;
I should not speak of it: it does not matter—
Not in the least.

#### Ina.

                  What matters anything,
In this blank desolation?

#### Dr. Lorne.

                  Don't now, Ina;
I sha'n't know what to do if you break down;
And people die, but still the world goes on,
And those who live must eat, and pay their bills,
And think of things.

#### Ina.

                  Ay! that's the pity of it—
To come straight from the shadows and the lights,
The awe and mystery and sacred sorrow
About the grave, to life's poor commonplace—
Not yet, at least, I cannot do it yet.

*Dr. Lorne.*

Well, no; but then I've seen so many drop—
Comrades and friends—and had to carry on
The battle or be beaten : one has hardly
Time here for feelings.

*Ina.*

May one come to that?
Were it not better not to be than live
To find no time for what is best in us,
What purifies and elevates and makes
A larger world than our small round of tasks?
Ah me ! a dreary outlook.

*Dr. Lorne.*

Not at all:
But for this business, now, no doubt it will
Be cleared up some day.

*Ina.*

What is there to clear?

*Dr. Lorne.*

Oh, nothing.  You must not be troubled yet
With business.  But your father now, he never
Went in for iron " rings " or " corners," did he?
And no sharp fellows ever talked him over,
And blew him up with hopes of boundless wealth,
Which by and by collapsed and left him broken?

*Ina.*

I do not understand.

*Dr. Lorne.*

Of course, you don't:
No more did he.  You never heard him speak
Of mines, I daresay—copper mines in Spain,
Or silver in Peru, and how they paid
Fine dividends?  No, no; you never did.
Yet parsons burn their fingers sometimes there.

*Ina.*

I have known papers come to him, which he
Flung in the fire, saying that it was well
He had no gold to gamble with.

*Dr. Lorne.*

Quite right;
One needs to know the game to play with these
Sharp fellows.  Well; no doubt, he never printed
A learned Book now—one that would not sell,
Was never meant to sell, but just to be
A splendid monument of erudition,
With costly illustrations, setting forth
Highland antiquities, and early arts
Now lost in their descendants, which he sent
To all the letters of the alphabet

Who voted him their thanks?  He might have
    done it;
But no, he didn't?  I'm at my wit's end now.
And after all, he could not drop that way
More than a thousand or so.

*Ina.*

              What do you mean?

*Dr. Lorne.*

Oh, nothing; never mind; I'm only stupid,
Let's talk of something else.  We're rich enough.
There; dry your eyes.  I don't suppose you could
Smile on me now to say I have not vexed you.

*Ina.*

Indeed you have not, uncle; but I wish
That I could clear up your perplexity,
Whate'er it be.

*Dr. Lorne.*

        No matter.  By the way,
Was not the Chief most kind to do him honour,
Bearing him to his grave with kilted men
And pipers, though I hate both kilts and pipes.

*Ina.*

Indeed he is a noble gentleman,
And held my father high in his esteem.
He was his pupil once—

B

*Dr. Lorne.*

              O ! and you learnt
Lessons together?—Latin and Greek and Hebrew?
'Twas all the old chap knew.

*Ina.*

              There you are wrong, sir;
O he knew many things, and taught me much
I now remember only to regret
I did not learn it better.

*Dr. Lorne.*

              That's the way
With me too.   What a deal I have forgotten
Since he and I were boys, and went to school!
Well; I must see the chief, of course, and thank
    him :
It is worth thanks, although that strutting piper
Looked like a turkey-cock, and yelled as mad
As e'er a wild cat.   After that we'll go
Off to Glen Chroan, and my house shall have
At last its mistress.   Never wind blew yet
But it brought luck to some one, though 'tis sad
My house is filled by emptying of his.

*Ina.*

You are most kind, good uncle.  But indeed
I have not thought yet what I ought to do.
It seems as if I could not think, for when

I try to knit my mind to any end,
My head goes swimming round, and all is blank.

### Dr. Lorne.

Yes, yes! I understand.  But there's no hurry,
Nor need of thinking either.  You may leave
All that to me.  You shall have pretty rooms,
And nestle like a dainty lady-bird
In a blush rose.

### Ina.

        That never was my dream
Of life; I'd prove a restless lady-bird.
I have my work to do.  Death sets one thinking
What to make of one's life—how best to use it.

### Dr. Lorne.

Work! O your mother's meetings, Sunday schools,
Sick-visitings, and mending poor folk's ways—
I wish they'd take a turn at mending ours;
We need it.  Well; our clachan is as like
A Sontal village in the jungle lands
As one muck heap is like another; filled
With lazy, hulking men, hard-featured women
Who slave for them, and ragged dirty children
Brimful of mischief, and original sin.
Work enough there to keep your hands full, Ina,
And see no end to it.

*Ina.*

That's very bad,
Have they no minister?

*Dr. Lorne.*

You women, now,
Think that a minister is everything,
That if you plant a parson on a moor,
He'll make an Eden of it just by dropping
His texts and preachments to the right and left—
Well, yes, there is a minister, but he
Is twenty miles away, and might as well
Be twenty thousand.  They are mostly of
The old Roman way.

*Ina.*

But there will be a priest then?

*Dr. Lorne.*

Ay, he comes now and then, and gives their souls
A hasty wipe that leaves them as they were,
Ere a week's over.

*Ina.*

And can you do nothing?

*Dr. Lorne.*

Me, Ina!  It is hardly in my line
To cast out Devils.  They'd turn and preach at me.
I give the priest his dinner, and the children
Pennies to wash their faces.

*Ina.*

Ah ! poor folk,
With none to care for them.

*Dr. Lorne.*

But now you're coming
Home with me, and they'll maybe do for you,
What is like sowing corn upon the rocks
Among the whelks and limpets, when I try it.
Ina, I can't say pretty things to you :
I've not a bit of sentiment in me,
And never had : I take my stand on facts,
And do not blow my feelings into bubbles
To see them break, and break my heart for them.
But see, my house is nothing but a house,
Till you shall make a home of it—a nook
Where the old dog may curl up in the sun,
And sleep away his age.

*Ina.*

But I have neither
The wealth nor will to lead an idle life.

*Dr. Lorne.*

Well, there is ample work in our wild Clachan—
Souls to be saved, and bodies to be healed,
And dirt enough to cleanse.  And as for wealth,
We'll ruffle it with the best, if that will please you.

*Ina.*

That is not what I mean.    We Highland maidens
Like independence, uncle.

*Dr. Lorne.*

O you'd rather
A trifle of your own than hang on me?
And so you should have had, and that is just
What puzzles me.    Your father made a will,
Only there was not anything to will
Except a squash of sermons.

*Ina.*

How could he
Have aught to leave, with only this poor parish?
You know his hand was open.

*Dr. Lorne.*

If his head
Had been but half as open to ideas!
But that was always shut, and his hand never.

*Ina.*

He was a good man, uncle.

*Dr. Lorne.*

Far too good.
There should have been a world made just for him,
Where no rogues grew, for never idle tramp
Whined at his door, I wager, but he fingered
Some of his coppers.    He was never wise.

*Ina.*

Yet goodness has a wisdom of its own,
And oft sees deeper than a shrewder wit.
And since I saw him lying cold and dead,
The idea of his life, which my poor breath
Had sometimes clouded, seems to come out clear,
And pure, and shining with a saintly beauty.

*Dr. Lorne.*

Yes, yes, a saint; but saints, you know, are not
For earth, but heaven.  I pray you, do not set
The pretty fountains of these eyes a-playing,
Or you shall quite unman me.  I'm at sea
About that will of his—that you should be
Left penniless, and even more, that I
Should somehow have been cheated.  Did you never
Hear of my being dead in India?

*Ina.*

Yes, years ago, and O how bitterly
He mourned for you.

*Dr. Lorne.*

    And yet I dare be sworn
He never said a prayer for my poor soul,
Although he feared 'twas in an evil case.
He might have risked the heresy upon
The chance of giving me a lift somehow.

No matter.   Was there nothing came to him
From India then ?

*Ina.*

No, nothing : but some debts
Of yours—they were not much—he had to pay,
Which pinched us for a while.

*Dr. Lorne.*

The Devil, it did !
Some debts of mine, and no memorial else
Of his dead brother !

*Ina.*

But you were not dead.

*Dr. Lorne.*

True ; but you see I was the prodigal
O' the family, and had eaten my swines' husks ;
And though I did not pine for fatted calves,
I thought of him, old fellow,—the elder brother,
Who was not a curmudgeon.   At that time
It suited my convenience to be dead,
Or to be thought so for a while at least.
I'll tell you more some day.   Old uncles, Ina,
Are mostly useful when they're dead ; and I,
Living, had been a sorrow to my folk,
A vagabond that had no touch of grace,
And now, it seems, my dying did no better.
Well ; I must see to this ; there's plainly some

Rogue-work to ferret out, and I will do it.
No money ! and even debts of mine to pay !

*Ina.*

Nay, do not think of them ; they were but trifles,
And cheerfully he paid them for the honour
Of your good name, and would have done far more
To know that you were living.

*Dr. Lorne.*

                                    But it looks
As if I had shammed death to get my bills
Settled for me ; and that is bad.  Moreover,
'Tis plain I have been tricked and overreached,
And that I can't abide, and never could.
They'll need their wits who play that game with me.—
I daresay now you did without a frock,
Until those debts were paid, and turned and trimmed
Old hats with faded ribbons.  My poor Ina,
You shall be dressed the handsomer for that,
There's plenty for us both, lass, at Glen Chroan—
Big empty rooms that will have ghosts betimes
If you come not to lay them, and a waste
Of meat and drink for lack of house-keeping.
Tis somewhat lonely too ; old faces flit
About i' the gloaming, that I'd rather not
Be seeing there ; and if you do not come,
I'll sell it, and be off again.  I'd rather

Squat by a jungle fire, and hear the tigers
Growl in the nullah than sit there alone,
With gnawing mice and memories.

*Ina.*

No, Uncle,
You must not go off wandering again,
Although a life of indolence and ease
Fits not my humour.

*Dr. Lorne.*

Busy idleness
Is just a woman's work.

*Ina.*

Nay, I hope not.
[*Exeunt.*

Chorus.

Did she speak wholly
Truth? Was it solely
Work that she wanted?
Ah! life was tame there,
Change never came there,
And who shall blame her
If she was haunted
With the young craving
For doing and braving
In the world's battle,
And weary of mountains,

Lakes, woods, and fountains,
And slow sleepy cattle?

But why should she linger
There, if this hunger
Gnawed so within her?
Was there another,
More than a brother,
Hoping to win her?
Ah, who shall blame her?
Life was so tame there
Until he came there.

## ACT FIRST.—SCENE THIRD.

### CHORUS.

Ah me! but Death is cruel to the living
    Left to dim outlooks, and to past remorse;
Cruel and cold is Death, and unforgiving
    The silent corse.

In the old home, now still and sorrow-stricken,
    She sits alone, and passions her sharp pain,

Fain to put from her aught that yet might quicken
        Her hope again.


Sweet scents are wafted from the clover blossom,
    Sweet songs are ringing from the earth and sky,
Sweet lights are lingering on the Loch's calm bosom,
        Far off and nigh;


The swifts and swallows, from the roofs and gables,
    Twitter their gossip in the evening light;
And the brooks, rippling o'er their glossy pebbles,
        Croon out of sight;


Flaming through curtain-clouds, the sun is shining,
    In gold and crimson wrapping sea and shore;
While she a subtle sorrow sits refining
        In her heart's core.


O empty home!  O dim and dismal chamber!
    O vacant chair, and book he left half-read!
O all the tender past, she can remember,
        Seared now and dead.


And from that dead past points a warning finger
    Bidding her 'ware of that which she loves most,
And on its silent lips the words yet linger—
        Love and be lost!

Scene—*The Manse Library.*   INA (*alone*).

## *Ina.*

What could it be? what could he mean?   Ah me!
That half-told tale, just broken off where all
The mystery was deepest, and the secret
Now left to mere conjecture!   All that night
My love did comfort me; that was not wrong;
God dropt it in my cup to sweeten it,
And I was grateful for it, and I thought
That it would comfort him too: so I told him.
But he said, "No; you must not love him, child;
Evil will come of it; I should have told you"—
But when he would have told me, I could hear
Only a whispered "Doris," and some sounds
But half-articulate; and then the awe
Of the dread change, the veil impalpable,
Inscrutable, came over him, and he
Carried the secret with him to the grave,
And I may ask, but can no answer have.—
They talk of spiritual forms that float, unseen,
Around our lives, and hands that feel about us,
And write on tables messages that mean
Nothing or anything—just as we wish.
But these are bubbles which the stream of thought,
Fretting against its limits and obstructions,

Throws up in its dark eddies.  There's nought in them.
What though my father haunted this old room
Where he kept company with other spirits,
Wise in their day, embodied in these books
So fondly read?  Yet if he spoke to me
I should not know if it were he that spoke,
Or my own fancy: and what were I the better
Of such a presence, if it only hovered
Silently in the unresponsive air,
And knowing all, could give no help at all,
Or speaking out, could work no faith at all?
Better for him "the better mansions" he
So loved to speak of, and not worse for me.
The misery is the silence; and the silence
Is never broken.  Death can hold its peace,
Let life go wailing onward as it may.
Ah me ! the mystery of it ! all is dark ;
Our little thoughts fly forth like gleaming sparks,
Hammered from our hot hearts, and straightway die
In the blank dark.  What meant that half-told tale,
And whispered " Doris " ?

Enter MORAG.

Morag.

                        Ina, shall I bring
The lamp now?  In the gathering dusk of gloaming
Our thoughts grow eerie, for their shadows look
Even bigger than themselves.

*Ina.*

Nay, this is best;
Fittest the sombre light for sombre thought—
The glimmer of a day that is no more
To brood upon the loved that are no more.
No lamp yet, Morag.

*Morag.*

Ina, you are wrong
To nurse this sad and melancholy mood,
To dream all day in settled loneliness,
To pass, untasted, dishes from the table,
To see no callers coming in all kindness,
To sit with folded hands and do no work,
To look with blank fixed gaze at these old books,
Yet reading ne'er a word, nor reading right
God's providence, but hardly judging Him
Because He does the best for us He can;
And that's not much.  The very stags that sicken
Casting their horns, yet make their profit of them,
Eating them up to make their bones the starker,
As we should with our troubles.

*Ina.*

Leave me then
To feed upon my sorrows, and in truth
They are hard eating.

*Morag.*

          And you'll find it easier
To pity yourself than to find out God's meaning,
Who throws His letters down, that we may put
This one to that, and turn them into words.

*Ina.*

Indeed, I am not pitying myself;
But the brisk current of my life is fallen
A-slushing among reeds and rushes.

*Morag.*

          What, then,
Has come of all your schemes for righting wrong
Among the Crofters and the Fisher folk?

*Ina.*

Dreams, idle dreams! vain dreams of fond conceit,
As fruitless as the dew-drops that are strung
On gossamer threads o' chill October mornings.
I am an idle and a useless maid
That heard the far-off rumour of the world
Beyond these hills, and hoped to plant its thoughts
Among the heather, where they will not grow.

*Morag.*

There's to be no more school, then, for the women,
To train them for their house-work, and to keep them
From bearing burdens women should not bear,
And dragging harrows too, like horses?

*Ina.*

                              Truly
They would not heed me, neither men nor women :
It was the way their fathers did; why should they
Change the old customs?

*Morag.*

                    And the new stone-pier
That was to make safe harbourage for the boats?—

*Ina.*

Waits till the lads are drowned, for they would rather
The people went away.  They told me girls
Should mind their seams, and practise at their scales,
Not meddle with men's matters.

*Morag.*

                         But the chief?
Will he do nothing?

*Ina.*

                    That I do not know :
They say he is not rich, save in a kind
And generous heart.  And O, the heart can do
So little, except—wish.

*Morag.*

            You give up hope then?
                    C

### Ina.

Morag, you've seen the Loch, on some still evening,
Mirror each stone, and twig, and tuft of fern,
And orange lichen on the rock, so clear
That which was substance, which was only shadow
You scarce could tell, till suddenly a breeze
Would blur it all, and there was nothing left
But dim confusion.  So it is with me now.
Once every thing looked plain to me, and truly
I did not well distinguish what was fact
And what was only fancy, and now all
Is like those shadows gone.  My heart misgives me
Since he has left me.

### Morag.

But why should it fail you?

### Ina.

I did neglect plain duties here at home,
And therefore met but failure out of doors,
And now I have no duties, and no home.

### Morag.

Ina, your heart is low, as one will be
Who sits down in a mist instead of stirring
To keep the blood warm.  Were you up and doing
You would be brisk and hopeful.  Are you meaning
To live now with your uncle?

*Ina.*

                    Wherefore not?

*Morag.*

They say there is no Sabbath in his house.

*Ina.*

Well; we could bring it with us.

*Morag.*

                    But they tell me
It's like a devil's Sabbath, or a Fair
With guzzling, clinking glasses, barking dogs,
And cursing drovers.

*Ina.*

                    Nay, he is not strict,
As we are here; but that can hardly be.


*Morag.*

And no one thinks of God but the black man
Who keeps an idol cross-legged, like a tailor,
Sitting upon a cow.

*Ina.*

                    Mere gossip, Morag;
But truly I am not enamoured of
My uncle's house, and sometimes I have thought
'Twere best if you and I could run away,
And find some simple home, and have a roof
For Kenneth till his student days are past.

Perhaps a woman has no fitter task
Than just to help a man to do his work.

#### *Morag.*

O Ina, I have dreaded you would go
To that old heathen, and I could not do it,
And yet I could not leave you.  But to live
With you and the boy Kenneth!  I will haste,
And write my cousin to look out for us
A house beside the college.

#### *Ina.*

Nay, there is
No hurry, Morag; nothing yet is clear.

#### *Morag.*

Pity that Lochs and Hills and Maids should be
So fickle!  It would be a happier world
If they could know their own minds half-an-hour.
But that they never do.

#### *Ina.*

Enough of me:
There is no armour but it has its joints,
And where the joints are there the arrow sticks,
And you who know me best know where to seek
My weakest points: and maybe I am fickle.
You cannot think more poorly of me than
I think myself.

*Morag.*

I don't think poorly of you,
Although I see your faults.  Why will you shut
The door to every caller, and sit here
As lonely as a seal in some sea-cave,
Or heron dreaming by a moorland burn?

*Ina.*

You would not have me lay aside my grief,
Which has its healing virtue, for the set
Phrases of cold condolence?  Who has called?

*Morag.*

Well; first there was Miss Doris.

*Ina.*

Do not speak
Of Doris.  When the heart is at its best,
And all its finer feelings tremulous
With some emotion it is bliss to feel,
There are some people—mostly women too—
Who touch the spring of what is worst in you,
As when you dream a happy dream, and lo!
A hideous face leers on you.

*Morag.*

Well; I say not
That you lost much by sending her away;
She's like a wasp whose drone has little sense,

But its striped tail can sting.  But then My Lady
Was with her.

*Ina.*

          Ay ! they always are together ;
The more's the pity.  Can she have some hold
On Lady Margaret ?  I've marked of late
A change in her—a kind of frightened look
And pleading way, and hesitating speech,
As if she would, but dared not.  Could I think
Of aught but my own troubles, she would be
A care to me.

*Morag.*

          But, Ina, you should think
Of other things ; for thinking of yourself
Is hardly thought at all : and when your head
Gives over puzzling, you will surely be
Just like the larch that, when it dies a-top,
Begins to die all through, and we may dig
A new grave in Isle-Monach.  After them,
We had a call too from the English ladies
At Corrie-Eylert.

*Ina.*

          O, they came to note
My way, my looks, and specially my dress,
And to retail the gossip as they went
Their round among the neighbours.

### Morag.

                    Let me tell you
Folks' hearts are often better than their habits:
They're sorry for you, but that's not enough,
Because you are so sorry for yourself.

### Ina.

That's a hard saying, Morag.  Can you think
My grief is for myself, and not for him
Whom I have lost?

### Morag.

            Why should you grieve for him,
Because he is in heaven, and has no care
Of writing sermons now, and is not so
Dead-weary of himself as when he sat
There at his table, scratching with a quill
To make words do what only thoughts can do.

### Ina.

Hush, Morag; 'tis not meet that you should speak,
Or I should hear such words.  He was my father.
You do not understand—you never did;
And O I am so lonely.

### Morag.

            You were nearly
As lonely while he lived as you are now.
If he had ever, like a father, watched

What books you read, what thoughts they bred in you,
What hours you kept, what friends you had, if any,
What schemes were shaping in your busy head,
Or even how you dressed!  But you might go
With any one, and anywhere, in rags,
And he would never notice.  And yourself
Have told me that he scarcely heeded aught
But Firstly, except Secondly and Lastly;
Write, writing, every day and all day long.

*Ina.*

I will not hear you, Morag, this is cruel,
At such a time.  If I was malapert,
'Twere fitter to rebuke than second me.
Moreover, when I said that, 'twas not he
I blamed, for he was good—O so much better
Than I—and still with conscience made his life
A sacrifice to duty, offering up
The sweetness and the gladness of it all
To what his office claimed of him.  It was
The exigency of mistaken work,
The rigour of a wrong idea planted
In a true heart that never spared itself,
Made me so speak.  But yet I spake amiss,
And rightly now am humbled.  Pardon me,
Dear father, that I judged you wantonly
In petulance of youth.  I had no mother.

Morag.

Scold me well, Ina; it will do you good.
I thought to rouse, and I have only crushed you.
Nay, spare me not, an old conceited fool!
Only you are my bairn.

Ina.

     There; go away.
I daresay you meant well, but there are sores
May not be touched but with a skilful hand,
Not with rough loving even.  You think I pity
Myself!  I hate myself, when I remember
The failure of my duty and my love
To him: and yet the burden of my sorrow
Is bound on me by what is best in me,
And when I part from it my good departs,
Therefore I clasp it to my heart of hearts.

CHORUS.

Ah me! but it is hard to hear
  The echo of your own wrong thought
  Which you were fain had been forgot,
Come jarring back upon your ear,
Come jarring back upon your heart,
  And smite it with a keen remorse,
  When you would shape a better course,
And hope to play a nobler part.

There, day by day, his hand would write
  New sermons, but the thought was old—
  Fresh-minting the same brass or gold,
And careful but to coin it right;
For with unshaken confidence
  He stood upon the old safe ground,
  And turned the problem round and round,
And still brought out the same old sense,

And hoped the world to overcome
  By rounding periods; and she said
  That it would be by sleep instead—
O better that she had been dumb!
For now it all came back again,
  The scratching of the patient quill,
  The paper that he needs must fill,
All changed into a choking pain.


## ACT FIRST.—SCENE FOURTH

### CHORUS.

All from the many-moulded door
On to the three-cusped window high,

Every stone on the pavement floor
    Marks where the chiefs and their kinsmen lie—
Dark slabs carved with the great Cross-sword,
    And the fish, and the galley, with scrolls all round,
And dim-lettered texts from the Holy Word;
    But all in the damp moss swathed and bound.


One sidewall long had in ruins lain,
    And O but the carved work mouldered fast
'Neath the suns, and the frosts, and the driving rain,
    And the tread of time as it hastens past,
And the seeds of life, and the wrath of man
    Casting down that which is fair to see,
Some day to grieve that he never can
    Bring back the glory that wont to be.


There at the head of the late filled grave
    Sadly a youth and a maiden stood,
And only the lap of the rippling wave
    Broke on the hush of their solitude;
Beautiful she, but as marble white,
    And looked like a monument planted there,
Till a broad beam of the garish light
    Smote with a glory her golden hair.

Scene—*Isle-Monach.*   INA *and* KENNETH.

*Ina.*

Thanks, Kenneth.   Now, I want to be alone.
Come back for me an hour hence.

*Kenneth.*

                              Yes, Miss Ina;
It is good to be here; yes, for there are
Good thoughts among the graves, and in the Islands;
Better than in the towns.

*Ina.*

                              What kind of thoughts?

*Kenneth.*

Well; dreams of peace, and memories of gladness;
And dreams and memories are all we have
To live on in the Highlands.

*Ina.*
                              You are sad;
What ails you, Kenneth?

*Kenneth.*
                              O these thoughts will come
When nothing ails you, as the clouds do when
The sun is brightest.   You will not stay long?

*Ina.*

No: but an hour is not too long to mourn
For a dead Father.

*Kenneth.*

        Yet it may be, Miss,
Too long to be alone here.  For these isles
Are hollowed by sea-caves, and when you sit
Musing alone, and hear the water rushing
Around you, and beneath, it makes your breath
Come quick with fancies.  I had once a cousin
Passed but a night on such an isle, and he
Nigh lost his wits ere morning, for he thought
That every streak of mist, and gleam of moonshine
Pointed and mowed and mocked and laughed at him,
So weird-like was the feeling of the place.

*Ina.*

O nonsense, Kenneth.  Are you superstitious
Like all the rest—and you a scholar too?
But I am not like you a poet, born
To see the unseen, and feel a pulse of life
Beating in brooks and rocks and sandy shores.—
You lost a friend in him who now sleeps here.

*Kenneth.*

I lost my hope in life.

*Ina.*

        Nay, say not so :
We've not so many here among our hills
With the rare gift of genius, and the love
Of letters, and of all things beautiful,

That we should let them pine away for lack
Of needful culture.  I am almost sure
My uncle will do as my father did,
And send you still to College.  How is Mairi?

Kenneth.

Mairi is gone to Doris Cattanach,
And lost to me.

Ina.

    Ah! that explains your gloom;
You have fallen out, and hence your thoughts are sad.
But how should she be lost to you because
She's with her cousin?

Kenneth.

     Can a maiden be
With Doris, and remain what I have dreamed?
Can the thaw come, and footsteps tread the snow,
And broad wheels grind it down, and leave it still
As when the white flakes trembled down from
  heaven?

Ina.

Kenneth, I fear that we are hard on her,
We judge a stranger by our home-bred ways,
Who, maybe, walks by other rule of right.
I blame myself at times.

Kenneth.

    And so did I,

Miss Ina, when I heard that she had taken
Mairi to be with her.  I said like you
Perhaps 'tis we that have not understood her,
And she has ta'en my little maid to make
A lady of her, as you take a wild-flower,
And plant it in a garden to enrich
Its life and beauty.  So I went to thank her.

*Ina.*

And found your Mairi still your pretty wild-flower,
Only with brighter hues.

*Kenneth.*

I found her not
At all.  She is too grand to see me now;
And Doris only mocked me.

*Ina.*

Nay, in that
You surely are mistaken.  She's a lady.

*Kenneth.*

And I am but a fisher lad.  But you
Shall judge yourself.  There was a little song—
A trifle like the shelfa's short bright note—
Which I had writ for Mairi once to sing,
And loved it, for my very soul was in it.
Mairi had sung it in the great house there,
And Doris made a comic rhyme of it,
And said it over to me—very clever,

And funny, but there was no heart in it;
Yet it was like my own—O very like;
Only the soul was gone.

*Ina.*

Ah ! that was cruel;
But Mairi did not know of it, be sure.

*Kenneth.*

Do you think so?

*Ina.*

Nay, I am certain of it.
She is a girl whom neither wealth nor arts will
Turn from the bent of truth.

*Kenneth.*

Thank you for that.

*Ina.*

Let nothing shake your trust in her.  Be sure
Suspicion murders love, and from its death
Come anguish and remorse.

*Kenneth.*

I will remember.

*Ina.*

And, Kenneth, when you make yourself a name,
As I am sure you will do, for your songs
Are like the murmur of the running brooks,
Or like the wind that breathes upon the woods,
And from each tree evokes a separate note

To make the woodland harmony, and all
So simple and true that they must touch men's
    hearts—
Then you will do this, Kenneth: you will make
These fisher's homes, which you do know so well,
Dear to the world by your recital of
The patience and the pathos of their lives,
The tragedies enacted on the sea,
And hunger of the body and soul alike
Where bread and books are scarce.

*Kenneth.*

              That I will, Miss;
But you, we looked to you to help us?

*Ina.*

                  Nay,
That is all past and gone.

*Kenneth.*

             Why is it gone?

*Ina.*

This is a man's work; I have been a failure;
And made his last days lonely whom I loved,
And did no good to any one, and now
My way of life must needs be far from these
Gray rocks and lochs and isles.—Ah !

    *Enter* SIR DIARMID.

    *Sir Diarmid.*

            How now, Kenneth?

I thought you never left your books except
To trim the boat, and set the lines.

*Kenneth.*

To-day, sir,
I had to row Miss Ina to Isle-Monach.—
Was it an hour you said, Miss?

*Sir Diarmid.*

Going now?
Well, do not trouble to bring back the boat;
I'll see Miss Ina home.

*Kenneth.*

Yes, sir.

*Sir Diarmid.*

Good-bye !
[*Exit* KENNETH.

Ina, forgive me that I followed you
Into your still retreat.  I saw the boat
Making the cove behind the mussel-crag,
And could not help it.  What a wealth of beauty
Gathers around these mouldering abbey walls,
Draped with pale lichens, and with graceful tufts
Of small-leaved ferns, and lovingly embraced
By the ivy, which they once upheld, that now
With reverence dutiful sustains and brightens
Their sad and tottering age.  What cunning hand
Carved these dark tombstones with their pregnant
    symbols

That speak a braver faith than skulls and cross-bones
And Time with scythe and hour-glass?  You were
    right;
Our fathers had an Art and a Religion,
A sense of beauty and a hope in God,
Nobler than ours.  Do you come often here?

*Ina.*

Sometimes.  O yes, the isle is very lovely;
And yet I love it more for what it hides
Than for the grace that hides it.

*Sir Diarmid.*

                  Ah! I know.
Forgive me.  You would rather be alone.

*Ina.*

Nay, it is I should beg to be forgiven:
The place is yours; but yet it holds my dead
Along with yours.

*Sir Diarmid.*

        And living as well as dead,
Our races soon shall mingle once again;
Shall they not, Ina?  It is not so long
Since the two streams were parted.

*Ina.*

              Yes; I know.

*Sir Diarmid.*

Yes! may I take that for my answer then?

*Ina.*

Nay, do not wrest my words.  I only meant
That we were once of the same stock, and still,
After our kindly Highland way, the river
Scorns not the stream that left to turn the mill
And grind the meal.

*Sir Diarmid.*

         But gladly welcomes back
The mill-race to its bosom, having been
A shallow and a stony brook without it.
O Ina, you will make an empty life
Once more a flowing river full and glad.

*Ina.*

This is no time or place for thoughts like these;
I blame myself for listening, standing here
Where I should know but sorrow.

*Sir Diarmid.*

         Why should you
Know only sorrow here or anywhere,
Who bring such joy to others?  When a wave,
Broken and spent, ebbs back, what should it do
But mingle with the new wave flowing in,
And swell its volume?  Should not love for him, then,
Whom you have lost now blend with other love,
And make an undivided absolute bliss,
To fill and glad our life?  Yet it is true,

This place is all too sombre; let us hence,
And get the sunshine round us as within.

*Ina.*

But there's no sunshine in me.  I am truly
A most unhappy maid; and what was said
Must be as if it never had been said.

*Sir Diarmid.*

You cannot mean it. Ina.  What is wrong?
Do you not love me still?

*Ina.*
                    Do I not love you?

*Sir Diarmid.*

Yet you can speak thus calmly of unsaying
All we have said.

*Ina.*
                    If it is best for you :—
I cannot cease to love you while I live;
Yet I can live, and have no hope in love.

*Sir Diarmid.*

If it is best for me !  But it's not best;
It is the worst and bitterest could befall me.
What is it, Ina?  Something troubles you.
You used to be a leal, true-hearted girl,
And frank and brave and not fantastical.
Have I done aught to vex you?

*Ina.*

                     No, indeed;
You have not changed to me nor I to you;
I never trusted you as now I do;
Nor felt before how desolate life will be
Without you.   Yet I came here now to make,
Over his grave, a vow that we must part,
Which well may be the breaking of one heart.

*Sir Diarmid.*

Nay, but of two hearts if it come to that.
Yet why should any hearts be broken, Ina?

*Ina.*

Listen : we had not told him of our Love—

*Sir Diarmid.*

It was his sudden illness, not my will
That kept me silent.

*Ina.*

                 Yes, indeed, I know:
But when he lay a-dying, I bethought me,
Not witting that the end could be so near,
That it might comfort him to know our bliss;—
And it is bliss, whatever come of it.
But O ! instead of comforting, it made
A stormy bar across the river-mouth
Of life to him, and trouble and alarm.

*Sir Diarmid.*

But why?

*Ina.*

He muttered, meaning to explain,
Something—but it was half-articulate—
And all I heard was "Doris."

*Sir Diarmid.*

Doris, said you?
Well, now my heart is light again, and I
Could laugh like children at a pantomime.
Why, how could Doris come between us two?

*Ina.*

I cannot tell; only he named her name.

*Sir Diarmid.*

But what has Doris Cattanach to do
With us and with our love?  And do you mean,
Ina, that you could give me up to her?

*Ina.*

That would be hard.

*Sir Diarmid.*

I'd sooner mate me with
A cloud, cram-full of lightning, hail, and thunder,
Or wed a polar bear, and sail away
Upon an ice-berg.  Think no more of this:
Perhaps he did not hear you right, or else
The mind was wandering, as it often does
On the dim verge of life.

*Ina.*

Nay, he said plainly,
" It must not be; you must not love him."

*Sir Diarmid.*

Well;
But that's past helping, Ina.

*Ina.*

Yes, I know.
But yet his broken words left this whole thought
Clear in my mind, it would work harm to you,
And that through Doris˙ somehow.   I am sure
That was his meaning.

*Sir Diarmid.*

Well, it is a riddle
That puzzles me to solve.   Shall we then shape
Our lives by their hard puzzles?

*Ina.*

No indeed;
But yet it would be selfish if I shrank
From a plain duty for the pain it costs,
Or clung to that which would bring hurt to you.

*Sir Diarmid.*

But what would hurt me most were losing you.

*Ina.*

Ah! life is very hard.

*Sir Diarmid.*
                    Nay, life with love
Is just the very best thing that I know.
Now think no more of this.

*Ina.*
                    If I were only
More worthy of you !

*Sir Diarmid.*
                    Let me judge of that :
You rate yourself too humbly : it is I
Should have my doubts of being meet for you ;
And yet I think Fate meant us for each other.

*Ina.*
But if I were to be a burden to you.

*Sir Diarmid.*
I want that very burden, cannot rise
Without it to the heights where I would soar,
More than the kite without its load of tail.
Come, Ina, cast these fears away, and speak
As on that happiest day of life to me
When first our lips were framed to tell our love,
And you did paint for us a restful home
Amid a busy life, like this old house,
What time the monks lived in it, and the folk
Learnt of them letters, arts, and piety.

You have a dainty fancy, and it made
A pretty picture.

*Ina.*

But it was not fancy.
O Diarmid, you may do a great work here
Where work is greatly needed.

*Sir Diarmid.*

Could I take
To work as much as sport, and had your help,
Perhaps I might.

*Ina.*

Nay, do not think of me ;
You need no help but what their love provides.
The people live in memories of the past,
And all their happiest memories cluster round
Those of your name and you.  They may be stiff
To men of alien blood, at times even false ;
But you have but to say, and they will do,
For all their hearts are yours.  O if you knew them,
And their pathetic faithfulness of love,
Rooted in ages past.

*Sir Diarmid.*

There, now ; 'tis good
To hear you speaking once more like yourself,
A Highland maiden for her clan and chief.

I love the people, and at first, I think,
I loved you for the love you bore to them.
But yet the task is hard.

*Ina.*
                    That I know well,
For I have failed.   And yet the hindrances
To good and noble action mostly lie
In our own bosoms.

*Sir Diarmid.*
                    May be.   But the clergy,
They hold the place which once the chieftain held,
And what have they made of it?

*Ina.*
                        They have made
A patient, orderly, and pious people,
According to their light.   But they have not
The place of eminence and influence,
Which love has kept for you.   Besides, our age,
The more its spirit is religious, cleaves
The more to secular forms, and will not take
Its shape from priests.

*Sir Diarmid.*
                    But you will help me, Ina?
Will be my inspiration if I try it?

### Ina.

What other inspiration can you need
Than to redress old wrongs, and help the growth
Of civil polity, and self-control,
And homes made glad by fruitful industry,
And to be compassed round by all men's love?

### Sir Diarmid.

There; every word you say but shows me more
How much I need you.  I am not a hero;
Only a Highland laird, as indolent
As all men are whose life is passed in sport.

### Ina.

And I but a weak woman; I can do
So little.  And their life is an old growth
Of time—a heritage of history,
Not shaped by their intention, nor to be
Fashioned, at once, by our new modes of thinking.

### Sir Diarmid.

Now, say not you are weak.  There's nought so strong
    strong
As a clear-sighted woman.  You shall even
Do with me as you will, when I may hold
This little hand in mine, and call it mine.

### Ina.

O Diarmid, are we right?  My father's words—
His last words, mind—

*Sir Diarmid.*

Were something about Doris :
And would you give me up to her?

*Ina.*

No, truly.

[*Exeunt.*

CHORUS.

What has come over the sunshine ?
  It is like a dream of bliss.
What has come over the pine-woods?
  Was ever a day like this?
O white-throat swallow flicking
  The loch with long wing-tips,
Hear you the low sweet laughter
  Comes rippling from its lips?


What has come over the waters?
  What has come over the trees?
Never were rills and fountains
  So merrily voiced as these.
O throstle softly piping
  High on the topmost bough,
I hear a new song singing,
  Is it my heart, or thou?

## ACT SECOND.—SCENE FIRST.

### CHORUS.

Fond of shooting, fishing, hunting,
　　Sound of bagpipe, drum, or fife,
Yacht and sail and flying bunting—
　　All the ways of savage life;
Sick of clubs and jolly fellows,
　　Play and pantomime and clown,
Novels bound in blues and yellows—
　　All the idle ways of town;
Tired of all the strife of Parties,
　　Solemn dinners, routs, and drums,
Public meetings where no heart is,
　　And a chairman haws and hums;
What shall youth do when the river
　　Has no pools where salmon lie,

And the sun is shining ever,
  And the trouting streams are dry,
And the grouse-cock gaily crowing
  Fears not either dog or gun,
And the partridge broods are growing,
  While the corn grows in the sun?
Weary he of fly and feather,
  Weapon shining on the shelf,
Weary of unchanging weather,
  Weary maybe of himself;
For he was not meant for daily
  Bringing basket full or bag,
Shooting grouse or capercailzie,
  Stalking of the timid stag.
What shall he do, weary-laden,
  If in such a vacant hour
He shall happen on a maiden
  Lovely as a sweet wild-flower,
With a noble nature truly,
  Pointing him to noble deeds,
Plucking up the thoughts unruly
  Growing in his mind like weeds,
Opening to his soul a grander
  Life than he has lived before,
As among the hills they wander,
  Or beside the grey sea-shore?

Ah ! the passion, all-constraining,
  That now lifts his heart above
Vacant mood and vain complaining,
  Lapt in bliss of early love !


SCENE—*Kildrostan.*   SIR DIARMID *and* LADY
              MACALPINE.

*Sir Diarmid* (singing).

"To Norroway, to Norroway,
  To Norroway owre the faem."

*Lady MacAlpine.*

Why do you sing that ballad ?  My old heart
Goes pit-a-pat to hear it ; like the merle
That sees a gled o'erhead.   Surely you are not
Tired of me yet.

*Sir Diarmid.*

               Nay, mother, not of you ;—
You're always pleasant company—but somewhat
A-weary of the weather which is bad,
Being so good, and of myself a little,
And of the world in general.

*Lady MacAlpine.*

                        Don't be silly.

*Sir Diarmid.*

I think I never was more sensible,
But to be sensible is to be dull;
All sensible folk are tiresome.  Have you heard
That ever any of our ancestors
Mingled their blue blood with a gipsy witch's?

*Lady MacAlpine.*

What do you mean, goose?

*Sir Diarmid.*

           Only this, that I
Am rather of their roving disposition,
And with the first crisp bursting of the leaf,
Or even while buds are only reddening yet
On the bare boughs, and primrose banks are bare,
Begin to feel a stirring in my veins,
As if I must be off into the woods,
And hang a kettle on a tripod o'er
A fire of sticks, and steal my own young hares.
Yet here is half the summer past, and still
I'm at the chimney nook.  Had I not been
A baronet, I should have been a poacher
In shabby velveteen, and had a lurcher
Close at my heels, and half my days in jail,
And half i' the moors and woods.  I wonder we
Can hate them so, they are so like ourselves.

#### *Lady MacAlpine.*

Don't talk so idly, boy; you let your tongue
Run off with what small sense you have.

#### *Sir Diarmid.*

　　　　　　　　　　　　　　But how
About that gipsy, mother?　I am sure
There must have been one in our family tree.
Was she dropt from it as a rotten branch,
Or christened Lady Margaret Merrilees,
Or Honourable Gertrude Jenny Faa
Of Hedgerow Elms, in Thieveshire?

#### *Lady MacAlpine.*

　　　　　　　　　　　Hold your peace.
Your ancestors were noble and high-born,
And mated with the best blood of the land.

#### *Sir Diarmid.*

Well, mother, do not frown at me; I do
But jest, and yet it was a foolish jest,
The birth of vacant brains.　Having nought to do,
I've seen you bring old rubbish from your drawers—
Scraps of brown lace, housewifes, and baby linen,
Buttons, old dingy letters, battered thimbles—
And litter all the room with them; and I

Being idle, throw the rubbish of my mind
About me too, and sorry stuff it is.

*Lady MacAlpine.*

Well, well; you might find matter for your jests
Fitter than those to whom you owe your being.
But now you'll stay at home.  'Tis weary waiting
Alone in my old age.

*Sir Diarmid.*

     Old age ! why, you
Are younger in my eyes and handsomer
Than half the girls I meet.  My little mother,
You never can grow old, your heart's so young,
While they are old i' their teens.  Yet I must come,
Only I would not leave you quite alone.

*Lady MacAlpine.*

But wherefore must you go?

*Sir Diarmid.*

     A promise, mother ;
Far rather would I be at home with you,
And after this I mean to spend my days
In sheer respectability, and go
Duly to Church, and play the justice too,
And lecture rogues and vagabonds, and sit
On Boards, and manage every one's affairs,

Like a true Chief.   But there's a College friend
Who worships Thor and Odin, when he tires
Of Zeus and Aphrodite and Apollo;
And I had promised he should see the land
Of Vikings and Berserkars, and the Fiords
From which their galleys oared to seek adventures.
So now he writes me he is coming here
To-day, and I must get the old yawl in trim,
And see if she will float to Norroway.

*Lady MacAlpine.*
A friend who worships Odin!   Why, the man
Must be a pagan.

*Sir Diarmid.*
                    Well; he rather is
A something of a pagan and a poet,
Yet no bad fellow, either, in his way.
He will not sacrifice the sheep or kids
Or horses; being æsthetic, he will be
Content with fruits and flowers and wine-libations.

*Lady MacAlpine.*
What do you mean?   Is that what young men learn
At College now?

*Sir Diarmid.*
                    Yes; some of them prefer
Boating or boxing, cricketing or hunting,

Lawn-tennis, or to drive a four-in-hand.
But the more studious mostly spend their terms
Seeking for a religion.

                    *Lady MacAlpine.*      .
                              Now you jest;
I know it by your look :—As if young men
Could leave their parent's homes without religion !
Why let this mocking fiend ironical
Cover your better thought?

                    *Sir Diarmid.*
                              I do not mock.
It may be that they bring up from their homes
Their cradle-faiths, but they are stript quite bare
Ere many months pass.  And besides, a man
May wish new clothes, who is not wholly naked,
May feel he has outgrown his baby robes,
May be ashamed too of his rustic fit,
And fain to dress his soul in the last fashion,
And wear it jauntily.  So we are grown
To be a sort of dandies in religion,
Affecting the last mode.  At present, we
Incline to Pagan cults, but are not sure
Whether is best the Greek or the Barbarian:
While some prefer pure Atheism to both,
And will have neither soul, nor other life,

Nor anything but organizéd dust
Which lives its day, and on the morrow is
Moral manure enriching other lives.

*Lady MacAlpine.*
Diarmid, you have not lost your faith?

*Sir Diarmid.*
                              Well, no ;
I have not found a better than my mother
Sung o'er my cradle.

*Lady MacAlpine.*
                    That is well.   Pray heaven
You hold to that.   I hear such dreadful things
About our young men now; and even the girls
Chatter half-atheism with as brisk an air
As if it were new ribbons they discussed.
There's Ina Lorne reads books would make my hair
To stand on end.

*Sir Diarmid.*
                No fear of Ina, mother ;
Her heart's all right.   And that reminds me now,
It was of her I meant to speak.   She is
Alone in that dull house, and for a while
You too will be alone : why should you not
Have her with you to cheer your solitude?

We are her kinsfolk, and I've heard you say
She makes a good day in a drizzling rain.

*Lady MacAlpine.*

She sees no visitors, keeps her room, and claims
The privilege of sorrow to be rude.

*Sir Diarmid.*

Nay, mother, rude she cannot be, and least
Of all to you.

*Lady MacAlpine.*

   Well, no: but what means this—
This new-born care for cousins who would scarce
Count kin save in the Highlands?  You're not wont
To speak so warmly of them.

*Sir Diarmid.*

     That is true;
For some are bores, and some are gossips born,
And some are butterflies, and some are wasps,
And some are geese.  But Ina's not like them.

*Lady MacAlpine.*

No; but she's somewhat flighty, is she not?

*Sir Diarmid.*

How mean you?

*Lady MacAlpine.*

         Well, she always has some new
Enthusiasm—some pet scheme or other,
To remedy the lot of our poor folk,
Which yet is ne'er the better for it.

*Sir Diarmid.*

                Yes !
Maybe ; and yet one likes her all the more ;
For if it be a fault, at least it's not
A common fault among our Highlanders.
We're not enthusiasts for the people's rights ;
More shame to us that she is so alone !

*Lady MacAlpine.*

But, Diarmid, what will Doris say to it?
They have not taken kindly to each other.

*Sir Diarmid.*

Why, what has she to do with it?

*Lady MacAlpine.*

                She'll think
It is her place to keep me company,
And will resent to see another here.

*Sir Diarmid.*

Why should it be her place? and why should she
Resent your choice of Ina?  And indeed
That girl is too much with you.

*Lady MacAlpine.*

                    But the time
Draws near; and you must first arrange with her
Before you go.

*Sir Diarmid.*

                    What time? what do you mean?
What is there to arrange with her?   O yes!
About her shootings—I will see to that.

*Lady MacAlpine.*

Her shootings! nonsense: 'tis about herself.

*Sir Diarmid.*

Now, mother, you are many fathoms deeper
Than my line goes.

*Lady MacAlpine.*

                    Did not your father tell you,
As he lay dying, how things stood between
Doris and you?

*Sir Diarmid.*

                    Well; he was very fain
That I should wed her some day, and I promised—
For that I saw his heart was set on it—
That I would try to love her if I could,
And wed her if I loved her, which I cannot.

*Lady MacAlpine.*

And was that all? was there no sterner hint
Of hard necessity?

*Sir Diarmid.*
            There was no more.

*Lady MacAlpine.*

O this is cruel, laying it on me
To blur a father's memory.  But you promised
To love her, and you'll keep your promise.

*Sir Diarmid.*
                                    What
Troubles you, mother?  You are strangely moved.
I said that I would love her if I could,
And I tried hard, but she would never let me.
Even as a girl she always spited me,
Threw stones into the pool where I was angling,
Tore down the nests I watched with tender care,
And rode my pony till she foundered him,—
Cruel as well as spiteful.

*Lady MacAlpine.*
                        A spoilt child
With that hot Indian blood in her untamed ;
But unripe fruit is bitter oft i' the mouth,
Yet mellows with the months.

*Sir Diarmid.*

But has she mellowed?
I could not bear to leave you here with her;
And Ina too so lonely.

*Lady MacAlpine.*

Never fear;
We shall do nicely.  And for Ina, when
You make your nest here in the old family tree,
'Twere well to feather it softly, not to plant
A thorn there for your mate.

*Sir Diarmid.*

But Ina's not
A thorn.  She's never sharp, and never stings
Like Doris.

*Lady MacAlpine.*

Dear, I do not understand
Why you should harp on Ina.  Let her be.
Her uncle's house, of course, will be her home;
He's rich and solitary.  If you have nothing
Against poor Doris but her childish freaks,
Would you for them neglect your dying father's
So earnest wish?

*Sir Diarmid.*

Nay, not for them alone.
Mother, no man, that is a man, would care

To catalogue a lady's blemishes;
To say, I cannot love her for her pride,
Yet love her less in her humility;
When she is bitter, I cannot abide her,
And yet I loathe her more, when she is sweet.
Ask me no more; indeed, I tried and failed:
Besides, I cannot offer to a market
That does not want my wares.

> *Lady MacAlpine.*

　　　　　　　　　There I am sure
You are mistaken, for she likes you, Diarmid.

> *Sir Diarmid.*

Then 'tis a liking that I do not like,
And never shall.  Were Doris the one Eve
In all the world, I'd rather, for my share,
The thorns and briars outside, and leave her Eden
All to herself, than company with her.
Have I not seen you frown with mingled shame
And anger at her reckless speech? for still
Her thoughts go naked, and are not ashamed;
Yet not from innocence.  You love her not,
And would not like, I think, to sit on nettles
What time my wife opened her mouth to speak.

> *Lady MacAlpine.*

I know she has her faults—so have we all:

But you might help to mend them.   And O Diarmid,
It must be.

#### Sir Diarmid.

What must be?   And also why
Must it so be?   You speak in riddles to me.

#### Lady MacAlpine.

Diarmid, you love your father's memory ;
Would you not rather suffer any loss
Than part with that?

#### Sir Diarmid.

Indeed I would.   But who
Can take from me the picture of his goodness,
Hung in the inmost chamber of my heart,
As men set up a holy altar-piece
For worship.   That he was mistaken about
This girl, harms not his memory to me.

#### Lady MacAlpine.

Ah me!  I wot not what to do.   This task
Should never have been left to me.   I tell you
You have no choice but marry Doris now.

#### Sir Diarmid.

I have no choice, for I have made my choice,
And would not have her, mother, if she brought
A kingdom for her dower.

*Lady MacAlpine.*

　　　　　　　　　Nay, hear me; let
Me tell the sorry tale.  Your father, Diarmid,—
'Tis hard to unveil the faults of those we love,
When death has hallowed love—in his hot youth
Had wasted his estate with cards and dice;
But when he won my hand, which brought much
　　　wealth,
He promised ne'er to gamble while he lived.
Happy our life was while he kept his word!
Nor did he break the letter of it ever,
Only the spirit, cheating conscience so
With words depleted of their natural sense.
Then came this Malcolm Cattanach from India,
A widower, with one child, and very rich:
He had been born a crofter in Glenara,
Was a contractor and a money-lender,
And there were strange things whispered about him—
I know not with what truth, of course, but men
Were shy of him who had been in the East,
As many here had been.—But 'tis too much;
I cannot go on with it.

*Sir Diarmid.*

　　　　　　　　　Quite right, mother;
Let Doris and her dubious father drop
Out of your mind; they only give you pain.

*Lady MacAlpine.*

Would that were possible! I must tell you all,
Howe'er it wring my heart.   He settled near us
In the next glen, and lived a sumptuous life,
Costly, luxurious, though his ways were coarse,
And with a splendour of colour hardly fitting
The sober grey of our dim Highland glens.
Your father took to him, although he laughed
At the peach-coloured liveries, praised his talent,
Quoted his sayings, hankered to be rich,
And live like him; and they were closeted
Often for hours together.  Until then,
He never had a secret thought from me;
But now he kept me in the dark, and that
Wounded and wronged my love.  It soon appeared
This clever, scheming man had led him on—
Who knew no more than I—to speculate
In foreign loans, and mines, and for the rise
And fall of markets; and he, all unskilled
To watch the turns o' the tide, bought in too soon,
And sold too late, and gambled all away.
Ah me! the weary days! the anxious looks!
The fretful temper! and the settled gloom
With the fell crash at last!

#### *Sir Diarmid.*

>             But why recall
> This story now, since, after all, we have
> Enough for all our wants?  What need to cry
> O'er our spilt milk, when all our pails are full,
> And the cow yields as ever?

#### *Lady MacAlpine.*

>             Wait a bit;
> One day he told me that my all was gone,
> And I, like you, said lightly, Never mind;
> We have the old home still, and our old love,
> Which none can rob us of.  But therewithal,
> He only looked the gloomier, and cursed
> Himself, his friend, and all the ravenous crew
> Of jobbers and promoters.  Then I said,
> Now, let us have no secrets; that has been
> The worst of all our losses, the decay
> Of that full trust that made us one indeed.
> Perhaps a woman's wit may find a way
> To mend things, or to bear them.  I was sore
> At his concealment, sorer than I said,
> For empty heart is worse than empty purse,
> And mine had been made vacant by neglect.
> But when I found that Malcolm Cattanach
> Had led him on and on, till every acre

And every stone o' the house, and every right
Of fishing, shooting, mining, were in bond
To him for moneys lent and lost, my heart
Utterly failed me.


*Sir Diarmid.*

                        Are we beggars, then,
On Doris' charity?


*Lady MacAlpine.*

                        Scarcely yet.  I have
My jointure, and I got a legacy
After your father's death.  Not otherwise
Could you have gone to College.


*Sir Diarmid.*

                              Had I known this,
I would not so have wasted all these years
In idleness, that might have yielded fruit
For wintry days.


*Lady MacAlpine.*

              I thought your father told you.
But that's not all.  There is another bond,

F

That if you claim her hand ere you have passed
Your four and twenty years, then she and all
Her gathered wealth are yours.

*Sir Diarmid.*

How, if I fail?

*Lady MacAlpine.*
That will be very ruin.

*Sir Diarmid.*

One word more.
What, if I ask, and she refuse my hand?

*Lady MacAlpine.*
To punish her he gives you back the land.
But she will not refuse.

*Sir Diarmid.*

I daresay not.
'Tis a hard case.  Has Doris known all this?

*Lady MacAlpine.*
Yes, years ago.

*Sir Diarmid.*

Ah! that accounts for much.
I must have time to think.

*Lady MacAlpine.*

                There is your friend
Just driven to the door; a handsome youth,
But yet a bit effeminate. I'll see him
At dinner time.

*Sir Diarmid.*

             It is unfortunate
His coming at this moment. But I must
Be civil, though my head is in a whirl.

                              [*Exeunt.*

CHORUS.

Vain for a man to think that he
    Can hide what a woman is fain to know!
Vain to dream that she does not see,
    Because her seeing she does not show!
He cannot lie with a guileless look
    Of innocence pure that falters not,
And she will read like a printed book
    The riddle of his most secret thought.
Well she saw where his love was given,
    Saw that her tidings had quenched his light,
Saw that he grasped, as if for heaven,
    A hope that would leave him in sorry plight.

And O that Ina might be her daughter!
  O the dread of his fated wife!
O the hopes that were writ on water!
  O her boy, and his shipwrecked life!


## ACT SECOND.—SCENE SECOND.


### CHORUS.

Ah! what to do if one should get
A tawny lion for a pet!
Or some volcano as a boon
To show the fireworks of the moon!
O terror of his playful moods!
O horror of its lava-floods!
So troubled and amazed were they,
So feared what he might do or say,
That youth fantastical whose wit
With the old Pagan cult was smit,
And stormed, in words that swing and swell,
Like changeful peal of a tripping bell,
Against the love that is divine,
And for the love inflamed with wine.

Daily their simple souls were shocked
With fleering scornful words that mocked
At Faith and Unfaith, nothing loth,
At God and Science, lightlying both;
But what the shallow heart believed
Of all it praised, and all it grieved,
Although he did his rating well,
'Twould need a wiser man to tell.
Still Zeus to him was Great and Mighty,
Still reigned the foam-born Aphrodite,
Still bright Apollo's arrows flew,
Still Dian brushed the evening dew,
Still Naiads haunted fount and brook,
And life was like a fairy-book:
Or Odin stern came back again,
And Thor, and noble Balder slain
By Loke's dark counsel, and the Tree,
Great Ygdrassil, of Mystery,
And all the Myths of ancient Night,
Myths of the dawn and growing light,
Myths of the earth, the cloud, the star,
And life and its eternal war.

SCENE—*Kildrostan Park.*  SIR DIARMID *and* TREMAIN.

### Sir Diarmid.

So we give up our cruise, then, after all?
'Tis well; for, as it happens, it would scarce
Have suited me to go.  You'll not regret it?

### Tremain.

Why should I?  'Twas a sudden fancy struck me,
And just as sudden left.

### Sir Diarmid.

      No other reason?

### Tremain.

What other would you have?  Must one have reasons
To knock down fancies with—a club to beat
The vapour off, that passes with a puff?
I choose to have my whims, and let them go
E'en as I list.  It is a folly, man,
A superstition of these modern times,
To be in bonds to reason.

### Sir Diarmid.

      As you like.
But there's a nice breeze tripping on the Loch,
Tipping the waves with foam.  Have you no fancy
To ride the white steeds in a merry gale?

*Tremain.*

Nay, that's all past.   I hate a boisterous life.
Give me the calm of Tempe where no wind
Blows on the vine-stocks roughly, and where love
Pants in the sunshine dreamily among
The lotus' leaves and asphodels.

*Sir  Diarmid.*

What then?

Are all those pictures of the bounding sea,
And billowy roll of life there, and your skill
With sail and rope and rudder in a storm
But so much moonshine?

*Tremain.*

Moonshine! surely no ;
But poetry of course.   O you dull fellows,
'Tied down to facts, you lose the half of life,
Missing its fancied part.   I sit and dream
Of lying in a pinnace with my love,
On a pard's skin, or carpet Eastern-dyed
Of gorgeous colours, with a cloudless sun
Inflaming every sense, as we look down,
And watch the pulsing globe, and tangled arms
Of myriad Medusæ.   Then I see
Ideal storms loom darkly, and the waves
Lashed into madness, which I master so

That by the sense of power we relish more
The soft delights of love.  But your wet ropes
And clumsy oars—faugh! they give blisters first
And then a horny hand; and life is lost,
By so much, when you lose a perfect sense.
'Tis needful for my Art that I should have
Nice touch and taste and smell and sight and
    hearing,
That through all gates may fine sensations pass,
Into my being, and enrich my life.

### *Sir Diarmid.*

Tush! man; you are not so effeminate
As you affect.

### *Tremain.*

      I never handled rope,
Nor held a tiller, nor yet mean to do:
A harp, even, blunts the finger-tips.  You think
To be effeminate is to be weak:
I hold that manhood only then is perfect,
When it has all a woman's delicate sense,
And absolute refinement, and will answer,
Like the wind-harp, in tremulous response
To every breath of fancy.

### *Sir Diarmid.*

      How then shall you

Employ your holiday?   Our ways are rough,
Nor do we fear to blunt a sense by use.

*Tremain.*

If I might just go on as now we do,
Bound to no method, held to no set plans,
Floating as Fancy wills, or Fate decrees!
Those hills are beautiful in the purple lights
Of evening, glassed upon the quiet Loch;
And weird-like are the wavering morning mists,
Tinted with rainbow fragments, like the glories
Which hover in the cloudland of old times;
And pleasant is the swaying of the boat,
And lapping of the waters; and I think
I could write something smacking of the life
Of the young world, while yet the gods were in it,
As I look round, and see the fisherwomen
Wade through the surf i' the twilight to the boats,
Each with her husband, or her sweetheart, maybe,
Borne pick-a-back.

*Sir Diarmid.*

A barbarous custom!   I
Have tried to shame the men out of these ways,
And do not wonder that you mock at them.

*Tremain.*

I do not mock at them.   I never felt

More tenderly to any ancient relic
Than to this fond survival.  Let it be.
Why drive your modern ploughshare over all
The fields of primitive custom, making them
As flat and commonplace as turnip fields.
Let it alone.  It is the antique symbol
Of woman's loyalty to love—a link
Uniting us with a more touching life
Of loyal service.  Had I but such a Naiad—
Only not quite so freckled and uncombed—
To plash her large limbs in the waves for me!

*Sir Diarmid.*

Never was such a plea for barbarism
Pleaded before.

*Tremain.*

   And yet as good a one
As you shall find for worshipping a maid,
Until she is a wife to worship you.
Why is it barbarous?  Was the Greek a savage,
When the fair princess, with her laughing maidens,
Washed the white linens in the sparkling brook,
And lovers lay upon the grass, and noted
The dainty feet that splashed the shining spray?

*Sir Diarmid.*

Well, you may play the lawyer for the nonce,

And draw me out from murky heathen times
Precedents of authority to bar
The way of progress.  But you'll not persuade me
The custom's not degrading.

*Tremain.*

Ay, in vain
We hope to master prejudice by reason.—
But how about this Doris you should wed,
And will not, though her acres are so handy?
What ails you at her?

*Sir Diarmid.*

This; she loves me not,
As shrewdly I suspect; nor love I her,
As certainly I know.  And when we speak
Of marriage, that's a point at least.

*Tremain.*

I know not;
I'm not a marrying man, though all my life
Is love and poetry, which mostly lose
Their glory at the touch o' th' wedding ring.
It is a quakerish thing connubial bliss,
Tame and slow-blooded, dressed in browns and greys,
And with no flash of passion in the eye,
Or flush o' the cheek.  Is she not beautiful?

### Sir Diarmid.

Truly; yet with a dangerous kind of beauty,
Beauty as of a panther or a snake,
Lustrous and lithe; or so at least she shows
To me who love her not.  Her father wedded
In the far East a Hindoo girl, and so
The daughter is not, like our Highland maids
Ruddy and large with amber in their hair,
But slight and supple, and the sun has dyed
Her cheek with olive.  Yet she is most fair.

### Tremain.

Ah ! now you interest me.  'Tis just the kind
Of beauty that I worship.  Helena's
Was dangerous, and the grand Egyptian Queen's
Who conquered the world's conquerors, and the sun
Had softly dusked the snow of cheek and bosom,
That chills our northern women.  There's no joy
Without the sense of danger; therefore men
Climb the precipitous mountains with a sense
Of tingling perilous gladness : and I hate
Your meek and milky girls that dare not kiss
A burning passion, clinging to your lips.

### Sir Diarmid.

Doris is not a Cleopatra, nor
Helen of Troy—she's just a Highland lady

Touched with an Eastern strain.   You must not liken her
To your wild-eyed Aspasias.

*Tremain.*

But you said
Hers was a dangerous beauty like the serpent's,
And that is what I like above all things.
Serpents twine round you, clasp you in their folds,
And charm you with a gaze that does not flinch;
Firing you as the many-husbanded
Helen was wont to do, till men would lose
The world for one brief rapture of her kiss.

*Sir Diarmid.*

I spoke too loosely: you misconstrue me,
So fancying her.

*Tremain.*

There's nothing else against her,
Except that dangerous beauty, which is only
The prejudice of people commonplace.
I like to play with adders.   I had one
I loved once as you love your dog, and had
Subtler communion with it, richer thoughts
From its uprearings and its wondrous eyes
Than you shall get from any noisy hound
With its rough shows of liking.

#### Sir Diarmid.

                              Well, I'd rather
My dog should jump on me, and wheel about
Barking for joy, than have an adder twine
Slow folds about me.   But tastes differ.

#### Tremain.

                                        Ay,
They differ; yet there is a worse and better,
For taste is the true test of character:
The crown of culture is a perfect taste,
Which lacking, men are blind and cannot see
The higher wisdom.   'Tis the want of it
That floods the world with stale stupidities,
And hangs a vulgar arras round the mind
Of misbegotten fallacies.   Tastes differ!
And so do faiths and policies, but yet
Their differences are not indifferent.

#### Sir Diarmid.

You need not rave about it, man.   I used
A common phrase, as one does current coin,
Not caring to ring copper half-pennies
Upon the counter.

#### Tremain.

                      Oh!   Yet I take leave
To doubt the taste that shrinks from such a girl

As you describe your Doris: that is all.
The kind of woman, bred of Christian cult,
Whom you call womanly, to me is watery—
A Ghost, a mist that chills you with its touch.
How changed from the grand creature Nature made
For joy, and music, and the giddy dance,
And glorious passion!  There's a story of
Pelagia, leader of the mimes at Antioch
On the Orontes; how she came one day
Up from the silvern baths with her fair troop
Of girls, all glowing with the flush of life,
And bounding with light mirth, and lures of love,
Like the young hinds what time the year reveals
The antlered stag freed from the down of his horns;
And as she came, arrayed in purple skirt
Of Tyrian, golden bracelets on her wrists,
And tinkling anklets, and the flash of gems
Upon her bosom, on her brow of flowers—
Lo! then an anchorite, dried up and baked
With dirt of some dim cave where he had burrowed
With bats and owls, looked wistfully on her,
And craftily assailed her with regrets
That she brought not her beauty and her joy—
Another Magdalene!—to serve his Lord:
Wherewith being touched, she turns a penitent,
And comes next day, and lays aside her robes

Of splendour, and her bright and joyous ways
So winsome, and in squalid garb arrayed
Of sackcloth, visits graves and lazar houses,
Pale as a lily—a shadow called a saint.
What think you now of such a work as that
To pleasure heaven with?  While the old gods lived,
A woman was the glory of our glad
And fruitful earth.  But now you make of her——

### Sir Diarmid.

I prithee, peace, man.  If I did not know
This is but spinning moonshine for the love
Of phantasy, and framing paradox
To seem original, I could be wroth
With such trash-speaking.  Interrupt me not.
What, if your leader of the mimes had been
A chaste pure maiden, daughter of a home
Where mother-love enfolded her in customs
As sweet as lavender, and that she met
Some gay apostle of the flesh, and as
His penitent, became——what you have known?
The world is bad enough, and false enough
Without such gloss to prove its darkness light.
The devil is up to that; and does not need
That you should make fine clothes for him to wear
When he goes masking.  Let this stuff alone;

Or weave it into verses, if you will,
For fools to read, although I used to think—
But that was in my youth's fond innocence—
That poetry should stir the best in us,
And give fit utterance also to our best
In rhythmic music.

*Tremain.*

That was not your thought:
'Twas but an echo you and others tossed
From mouth to mouth, and thought that you had
    thought.

*Sir Diarmid.*

Echo or living voice, the thought is true;
God gives us song to make us nobler men
And purer women.

*Tremain.*

Nay, for art is not
The slave of virtue, turning songs to sermons;
But it is free, and is its own excuse,
And finds its purpose in its exercise.

*Sir Diarmid.*

What do you mean?

*Tremain.*

This.  Picturing truly all
Ideals—good or evil, as you call them—

G

Art doth fulfil her office, but comes short
Of her vocation when she aims at aught
But perfect form and colour and harmony.

*Sir Diarmid.*

Enough: I did not count on getting such
Art lectures from you.   Keep them for the freshmen.

*Tremain.*

You make a pedant and a pedagogue
Of that which is the sovranest thing in nature,
The freest and the gayest.   Out upon
The tyranny of small moralities,
Shop-keeping ethics, Pharisee respects!
As if high Art must minister to them,
Like a fair tablemaid who must not speak,
But let them prose and prose!   I hate it all.
For evil and good, yea sense and nonsense, Art,
Soaring above them in her own bright realm,
Yet lifts them up, and blends them in her charm
Of light and music and divinest vision.
But you are still in bonds to commonplace,
And cannot bear this yet.

*Sir Diarmid.*

                    Nor ever shall,
Nor ever wish to.   One might land in Bedlam
For less conceit of wisdom.

*Tremain.*

By the way,
There's one thing more I wish to know.   Last night,
Or rather in the gloaming, as you have it,
Upon the heights, beside the waterfall
That wavers like a tremulous white veil
Of bridal lace to hide the moss-clad rock,
I had a vision of beauty.

*Sir Diarmid.*

O belike,
The purple glow was on the hills.

*Tremain.*

Nay, but
A maiden passed me tall and beautiful,
Robed all in black.   Her step was like a queen's,
Pallas-Athene had no statelier mien,
Broad-browed, large-eyed, and with the confidence
Of strength and courage in her.   Who is she?

*Sir Diarmid.*

How should I know?   No matter.

*Tremain.*

Girls like that
Can't walk about the shores incognito :
You surely know her; think of it again.

I did but pass some pretty compliment—
Thrown at her, to be picked up if she chose,
Not spoken to her—an impromptu verse
That sprang up to my lips at such a vision
Of might and beauty delicately mixed,
When she, just pausing, gave me such a look,
As if she could have tossed me o'er the crag
Into the pool, then leisurely swept on.
Who is she?   All the fisher folk would say
Was, It will be Miss Ina.

*Sir Diarmid.*
                        Ay, that was
Ever her favourite walk.   Now, if you chance
To meet her there again, best let her pass
Without impromptu verses.   You might find
They breed unpleasant consequences.

*Tremain.*
                                    But
Who is she?

*Sir Diarmid.*
            Well; no matter: my kinswoman.
Her father was our pastor, lately dead—
No more of her.   When shall we visit Doris?
She's far more to your taste.

*Tremain.*

                    O when you will.
But that dark-robed Pallas-Athene—your
Kinswoman, said you?

*Sir Diarmid.*

                    Surely you would not
Intrude upon the sacredness of sorrow
Like hers.

*Tremain.*

        The parson's daughter—

*Sir Diarmid.*

                        Sir, I tell you
She shall not be molested.

*Tremain.*

                    So: I see
Why Doris' beauty is so dangerous.
Pallas-Athene broad-browed, shining-eyed,
That is your style, is't?                    [*Exit.*

*Sir Diarmid.*

                    Pshaw ! why should I care
For that fool's babble? for a fool he is
With all his genius, which is but a trick
Of stringing words together musically.
How could I ever bring him to the home
Of pious, pure-souled women.   Yet he'll serve

My purpose, if he only take to Doris,
And she to him—she is not over-nice.
But is it fair that I should plot and scheme
To save myself from a detested fate
By luring her into as dark a snare?
Nay, but I only bring these two together,
And by the mutual attraction of
Their kindred natures let them coalesce,
If so they will—and surely so they will:
Only the time is short.  Yet such folk jump
Into their loves; and if it so befell,
My path were clear, and all should yet be well.

CHORUS.

O cunning schemer!
O idle dreamer!
With crafty head,
And heart elate,
Spinning a thread
To baffle Fate!
Twirl the spindle ever so fast,
Let the thread be ever so fine,
Fate will rend thy web at last,
Fruitless labour surely thine.
Sore against thee are the odds
Wrestling with the immortal gods.

## ACT SECOND.—SCENE THIRD.

### Chorus.

Once more, with a heart undivided,
  And vexed by no discords of thought,
  But calm in the hope she had got,
In a great peace she abided.
Not that the grief was forgot,
  Or self-reproaches were ended,
  But that the sorrow was blended
With love, and the bliss which it brought.

Once more, like a dainty bird preening
  Its feathers, she cared for her looks,
  And pondered her favourite books,
And read with clear sense of their meaning;
And the fishermen, plying their hooks,
  Would hear in the dusk of the gloaming
  A full-throated song that was coming
From the Manse 'mong the trees and the rooks.

Once more, from her Dante and Goethe
  She came into clachan and cot,
  And still it was sunshine she brought,

Though her speech was of patience and duty ;
For O but she never forgot
The grace that is due to all human,
Or the low soft voice of a woman
Perfect in feeling and thought.


Scene—*Street: Post Office Door.*   Ina, Mrs. Slit,
Doris (*in the distance*).

### Mrs. Slit.

Goodbye, then, Miss Ina ; and it iss a light there will be in the shop this day, because you have been in it again.

### Ina.

Goodbye.   You will be sure to remember the warm things for old Elspet's rheumatism.

### Mrs. Slit.

Och ! yes, I will remember them.

### Ina.

And Dugald's snuff, and Alisthair's tea.

### Mrs. Slit.

And the snuff and the tea, though it iss the porridge that iss good enough for him, and more than he deserves, for it would be the whisky that brought him to this.

*Ina.*

Maybe.    But who of us get just what we deserve?

*Mrs. Slit.*

That iss true.  Yes! Some get more, and some get less ; some have a penny's worth for their halfpenny, and some only a farthing's worth for their penny ; and it iss the scales of Providence that would not do for a shop, whatever.  But I will mind, Miss Ina.

*Ina.*

That is right.    But there is Sir Diarmid's yacht in the Loch.    Is he going a trip anywhere?

*Mrs. Slit.*

Och! it iss that Poet-man that gets the letters and the printed papers every day.  He will not be for leaving the Loch, I think.  They are saying he iss a great bard or Seannachie, though I never heard him sing, or even whistle, as our lad Kenneth will do.

*Ina.*

But Poets make songs, and other people sing them now.  However, I must bid you goodbye now.

*Mrs. Slit.*

Goodbye ; but it iss Miss Doris that will be coming along the street now ; and which iss more, she will

be picking her steps, and sniffing as if her father
would be a chief instead of a cottar's son.   Maybe
you will not be caring to see her.

#### Ina.

Why should I not wish to see Doris?   But even
if I did not, I cannot help it now, for she has
seen me.

#### Mrs. Slit.

Fare you well, Miss.   And take care of that one.
It will be easier dealing with Elspet's rheumatics than
with her smiles, which only show her teeth.

#### Ina.

Good morning, Doris.   You are early astir.

#### Doris.

Well, this is pleasant, Ina, seeing you
Abroad, and like yourself again.   They told me
Your eyes were red with weeping; but they're not.
Indeed, I think they never were so bright.
That's right.   What is the good of injuring
The very feature of one's face that men
Chiefly admire?   One ought to think of that.

#### Ina.

Ought one?   I don't know that I did think of it.
But never mind: my eyes are all right, Doris.

### *Doris.*

That's plain enough to see; you look quite brilliant.
But how did you get through the time of mourning?
Is it not horrible—the blinds, the silence,
The people whispering, the dismal looks?
I was so sorry for you, and I called
A score of times, I'm sure.

### *Ina.*

                    I'm vexed at that ;
The servant only told me about once.

### *Doris.*

O twice, at least.   But then I meant to come
So often, and you would not let me in ;
Indeed, I thought of you from morn till night,
And could not keep you from my sleeping dreams,
I was so grieved.   How did you pass the time?
You don't read novels; yet they're such a help
At such a season.   Why, I lay all day,
And got through half of Mudie when my daddy
Dropt from his perch.   I can't think how you did.
It's dreadful to be shut up with the Bible,
And Pilgrim's Progress, just like prisoners
Upon the silent system.

*Ina.*

Well, I was not
Condemned to that quite, though I might have had
Worse company.

*Doris.*

You did not think of cards,
I daresay; yet you've no idea how
They get you through the evenings, when your heart
Is like to break.

*Ina.*

No, certainly I did not.

*Doris.*

Well, it's a pity now; for they just give you
The kind of mild excitement which you need
When you are low—not staking much, you know,
Only what will give interest to the game.
And when I called that day I meant to try them,
In case you had been very bad.

*Ina.*

O, thanks;
I daresay you meant kindly, but you do not
Quite understand me.

*Doris.*

Yes, indeed I do.
I hear folk say they cannot comprehend you,
But that is their stupidity, and I
Tell them I see you through and through like glass;
You are so simple.

*Ina.*

Oh!

*Doris.*

And when you shut
Your door, and would not see a visitor,
I said it was the proper thing to do,
And when the proper time came you'd appear
Splendid as ever; and there you are, my dear,
A miracle of beauty.  That dress, now;
You cannot think how perfect you are in it.
Where was it made?  But all your dresses fit you.
Was this what smote Tremain?

*Ina.*

What do you mean?
Who is Tremain?

*Doris.*

Not know Tremain! and he
Raving about you as a heathen goddess—
Not Venus, but another quite as handsome,

And cleverer far, though I forget her name.
Why, what can Diarmid mean, that he has never
Brought him to see you?

*Ina.*

            O, I am not seeing
Strangers at present.

*Doris.*

            But he's quite a genius,
And one should see them when they come one's way,
Which is not often; then he is so handsome,
And knows so many people, and is so
Charmingly wicked—but you'll not like that
Of course, because you've grown up in a Manse
Where every one is bound to be good, of course.
Tremain is quite a pagan, but his gods
Are all dead long ago; and he knows that,
And does not worship Zeus and Aphrodite,
As he would like to do; only he rages—
Ever so eloquent and beautiful!—
At those who overthrew their shrines and altars.

*Ina.*

Doris, you surely do not lend an ear
To one who, for the living God, would thrall you
To these poor bodiless shadows.  He must be
A shallow fool, I think; for there are some

Whose genius, like a marsh-light, flickers where
There is no footing for a man to go.

*Doris.*

But you know, Ina, I am only half
A Christian, half a Brahmin, and a daughter
Goes with the mother mostly, and I like
The folk you call poor heathens.  What he says,
Besides, is that it does not matter much
About our gods, whether they are or are not,
Or what they are.  The one thing that concerns us,
Is the idea of life which they call forth,
And ours is now all wrong.  The Church, he says,
Has consecrated grief instead of gladness,
Has cast the shadow of the cross where heaven
Poured down the laughing sunshine; even science,
That scorning miracle is full of wonders,
Potters o'er facts and numbers, and makes man
No more than a machine for grinding meal.
But the old gods of Greece made joyous life
With song and dance and flowers and wine and love—-
O you should hear him, just.

*Ina.*

Do you think so?
I fancy that a cross which tells of hope
Through sorrow, is better than remorseless fate
Chaining the soul to rocks and piercing ice.

I wish folk had more pleasure in their lives,
More flowers and sunshine, though I'd rather not
More foxglove, hellebore, and deadly nightshade.
What does he say of conscience?

*Doris.*

Conscience!  O
He thinks it is a blister that has made
The soul so sensitive it cannot bear
The touch that nature meant us to enjoy.
He's very scornful of it.

*Ina.*

So I fancied
The trifler would despise its inspirations.
Zeus never had much conscience.

*Doris.*

Then he brings you
Just to the verge of shocking things, and when
You're bridling up in anger, 'tis such fun
To watch him sailing off, as if he had not
Seen the improper thoughts which made you blush.

*Ina.*

And does Sir Diarmid like a man like that?
I cannot think it.

*Doris.*

They're inseparable.
'Tis strange he has not brought him to the Manse.

*Ina.*

Nay, it were stranger to have brought him there ;
Its air would not agree with him.

*Doris.*

Indeed,
He's quite a revelation—something new
Entirely in these parts.

*Ina.*

Yes, I should hope so.
A revelation—only of the darkness,
Not of the light.  I think I saw the man
Once, and I took him for a coxcomb truly.

*Doris.*

O, but he raves of you.

*Ina.*

That's likely enough :
His words are mostly ravings.

*Doris.*

No, indeed ;
He has the daintiest fancies, beautiful,
Poetic ; and he makes you gasp for fear
Of what he may say next, which is so nice.

*Ina.*

Is it?  I'd rather walk where footing is sure

Than on the thin and perilous bending ice.
But as you will: he does not interest me.

### Doris.

That's odd; I think I never met a man
So interesting, so fresh, and so mysterious.
Don't you like mystery in a man?

### Ina.

                I like
Truth, Doris, first, and reverence, and manhood;
And the true man is reverent to all women.
But now adieu. I am not given to preach,
And young men, they do say, are not like us,
Though why they should not be, I do not know.
But Doris, were I you, I'd hold aloof
From one who grazes improprieties,
And does not blush to make a woman blush.
Farewell.

### Doris.

        Where are you going, Ina dear?
O, to Isle-Monach? Yes! 'tis natural
You should go often there, and Diarmid too
Visits, of course, the graves of all his fathers.

### Ina.

I have been once there, Doris, since I laid

My dead in it; and if Sir Diarmid goes
Often, I cannot tell.

### *Doris.*
I fancied you
Might have met, now and then, by chance of course,
Where there is so much to attract you both—
A common feeling for your common kin.
But then he is so busy with his friend
Whom he admires so warmly, dear.   Adieu.

[*Exeunt*

### CHORUS.
Not for a moment distrustful
  Was she at all of her lover;
Yet, as she listened, a shiver,
  As from a cloud passing over,
Chilled her, and darkened the glory,
  Radiant, shining above her.

Doris she knew to be cunning,
  False too, and deft in her malice,
Clever at brewing of poisons,
  Secret, to drop in the chalice;
And she had masques, like a player's,
  Carefully stowed in her valise.

No, no, she did not believe her—
    Yet was the sting there remaining:
O no! her lover was noble—
    And yet it was rankling and paining:
Who could abide in such friendship,
    And keep from the taint of its staining?

# ACT THIRD.—SCENE FIRST.

## CHORUS.

Where the ancient sacred Ganges
    Slowly eats its crumbling bank,
Where the brindled tiger ranges
    Nightly through the jungle rank,
Where the hooded cobra sleepeth
    Dreaming of its victim's pang,
And its deadly venom keepeth
    'Neath the folded hollow fang,
In a city many-towered
Was a garden gorgeous-flowered,
And a marble-builded mansion
    Stood upon a terrace high,
Overlooking the expansion
    Of the garden's greenery.

There the Eastern sun, combining
With the Northern snow, entwining
Subtle brain and passion hot
With the will that bendeth not,
Made a woman strongly daring,
  Reckless in her self-reliance,
  Wanton in her world-defiance,
Little loving, and all unsparing.

Far away now from the sacred stream,
And the land that was growing to her like a dream,
Beneath the stars of a moon-filled night,
The lady sat in a chamber bright,
Scented with odours and flooded with light.
A cloth of gold for her seat was spread,
A leopard's skin at her feet was laid,
A jewelled fan was in her hand,
  And golden filagree in her hair,
And all about her was rich and grand,
  Of ebon and ivory, carved with care,
  And gorgeous feathers and carpets rare.

  Ah ! the smiling sacred river
    Carries death upon its wave,
  And the slumbrous cobra ever
    Wiles like the devouring wave,

And the brindled tiger ranges
    Through the darkness for a prey—
Tiger, cobra, corpse-laden Ganges,
    What do ye with a lady gay?


SCENE—*Boudoir in Cairn-Cailleach.*  DORIS *and* MAIRI.

### *Doris.*

Mairi, you are a fool.  If you were quit
Of these poor kinsfolk in Glenaradale,
Think what you might be.  You are very pretty,
And lady-like, and have the trick of dressing,
And matching colours—you might wed a lord
Who did not know the root from which you sprung.

### *Mairi.*

I do not wish to wed a lord, Miss Doris,
I do not wish to hide from whence I came;
I am a cottar's daughter, as your father
Rose from a like beginning.

### *Doris.*

              There's no need
Reminding me of that; but never mind,
After this week I'll hear no more of it.

*Mairi.*

But they will hear in heaven, where poor folks'
    prayers
Do fill its courts like incense.

*Doris.*

               Then you mean
To pray for vengeance on the friend who tried
To lift you from the mud.  O but you are
A proper saint.

*Mairi.*

          Nay, I am not a saint,
But, Doris, we might both be better women.

*Doris.*

Well, when I pray, for I am more forgiving
Than you, I'll pray for you that you may get
A better husband than that Kenneth Parlane,
Who'll starve you on his rhymes and rebuses,
Rehearsing them to clowns in alehouse parlours,
Inspired of usquebagh,—meanwhile his wife
Will time her poet with a tambourine.

*Mairi.*

You do not know him, Doris: but no matter;
Why should we part in bitterness?  You meant
Friendly by me, although your way of life
Cannot be mine.  "The sea hides much," they say,
And there is much that love will hide away.

*Doris.*

E'en as you will.   But here's another coming;
Adieu !

*Exit* MAIRI.   *Enter* TREMAIN.

*Tremain.*

Why, Doris, what a pretty maid
You have !   But beauty still should wait on beauty.
You need no foil; twin stars are doubly bright.

*Doris.*

How have we grown so deep familiar,
Who scarce have known each other for a week ?

*Tremain.*

A week ! I seem to have known you all my days.
The years before, like childhood, are a blank.
How did I live then ?

*Doris.*

O, like other babies,
Getting your milk-teeth, squalling now and then,
Making a noise with spoons, and being petted
And spoilt by kissing women.   What of Diarmid ?
Where is he ?

*Tremain.*

Well ; he's busy with affairs ;
A man of acres he, and beeves and sheep,

With tenants, gillies, keepers, and what not
To see to.

*Doris.*

Oh! He did not use to be
Quite so full-handed.

*Tremain.*

Then, he's not in love;
And no one cares to look on when a game
Is played by others, after he has thrown
His own cards up.

*Doris.*

He palms me off on you, then,
Having no taste for such poor gear himself,
Or else another market for his wares!
'Tis very well, Sir Poet.

*Tremain.*

Nay, I said not
Any rude word like that.

*Doris.*

Did you not tell me
He had thrown up his cards, and did not care
To see you play his game? So you have come
To take his cast-off, and relieve his mind
Of its perplexity! A gracious office!

Sure, gentlemen are most accommodating!
And doubtless I am honoured, could I see it,
And doubtless you are favoured, when you think on't!
People keep poets sometimes—do they not?—
For their own uses, as to praise their wares
In rhyming advertisement quaintly fancied,
Or to relieve the tedium of their greatness.
So I have heard.   But 'tis a new vocation
To take their leavings.

#### Tremain.

Ha! a clever shot,
And yet a miss.   How you do drop on one,
As a lithe panther lurking in a tree,
Licking his lips, with slowly wagging tail,
Might leap down from his branch, and bite the nape
Of the stag's neck, while every claw is dug
Into the quivering flanks.   I like to watch
Your eyes at such a time, at first so sleepy
With half-closed lids, then flashing out so fierce
With sudden lightnings.   You have the perfect art
Of deadly wounding; yet I am not hurt.

#### Doris.

A pachyderm, perhaps, or armadillo
Wearing his bones outside.   Some people have
An armature of vanity as tough

As the thick folds of the rhinoceros' hide,
And wot not when they are shamed.

### *Tremain.*

　　　　　　You miss the mark,
Though you aim low—or just because you aim
So very low.  I feel when I am hit
Like other men, and may be hit like them;
But then my feet are not among the dirt
To be hurt there.  So you have sped your bolt
Wide of the mark.

### *Doris.*

　　　　O yes! you are a poet,
And fly, of course.  It is among the clouds
That one must speed an arrow after you.
But whether you are singing lark, or gled,
Or  mousing-owl,  who  knows?  You  bring  such  strange
　　strange
Reports.

### *Tremain.*

　　　A lark, be sure, the bird of heaven—
A lark full-throated up in the blue heavens,
That all day singeth to his love below,
And only can be silent by her side.—
But what reports mean you?

*Doris.*

    Something you said,
Self-satisfied, about a laggard wooer,
A gamester who threw up his cards, and left
The play to you who gladly took his place;
I the poor stake.

*Tremain.*

    But not his cards I play,
Nor yet his game, whate'er it may have been;
'Tis my own luck I try, laying my life
Upon that stake.

*Doris.*

    Just so; he throws me over,
And then you take me up; he's done with me,
And therefore I am fit for you.  Perhaps
You like the game: I cannot say I take
The humour of it.

*Tremain.*

    Nay, it is not so.
I said he did not love you, which is true;
He said you loved him not, which I believed;
And so, because the way was clear for me,
I said I loved you, which is truest of all:
And I will challenge in the tournament

Of song all poets in the land to match
My Queen of Beauty—or be hushed for ever.


*Doris.*

Fine words !  But that's your trade.


*Tremain.*

                    Words !  If you knew
The passion burning in the heart of them,
The sense of utter weakness in all words,
In paradox and high superlative,
To speak the thoughts that swell and surge in me !
Listen a moment, Doris.  When I came
Hither to gather pictures and sensations
Among the mountains, and beside the sea,
And from dim caves, and from the whish of pines,
And lingering mists, and from the setting suns,
That I might write a book which should entrance
A brain-fagged world, then I was studying words
To trade on them.  But having lighted on
My Helena, my Fate, I heed no more
The hills, the lochs, the caves, the forest trees,
Or trailing mists, or glory of the sunsets,
Or curious felicities of speech,
Or swing of rhythmic phrase, or anything
But just to love thee, and to win thy love.

*Doris.*

There; that's enough; I half believe you, though
I fear I should not even half believe.
I think you love me just a little.

*Tremain.*
                                        Doris,

A little ! I am all, and over all,
Within, without, in heart and brain, afire
With a consuming passion which no sea
Could quench, but it would make its waves to boil
Though they were ribbed with ice.

*Doris.*
                                You've studied well
The art, at least, how one should play with hearts.
Yet if I were to prove your love with some
More simple test than boiling seas of ice,
It would not much amaze me though it failed.

*Tremain.*

Nay, put me to the proof; and if my life—

*Doris.*

Pray, let your life alone ; men wager that
Most freely, when they least intend to pay.
But if you cared to pleasure me, you could,
And I could love the man who pleasured me
As I would have him.

*Tremain.*

     Only tell me how,
And if a heart's devotion, and a will
Resolved, and some small skill of nice invention
To frame such dainty plots as poets use
To work out fates with, can accomplish it,
Count it already done.

*Doris.*

     I hardly know
How I should put it.  There's a girl you know,
At least you've seen her—Ina at the manse,
I hate her.

*Tremain.*

   Well then, I will hate her too.

*Doris.*

Nay, that is not my meaning.

*Tremain.*

     Then I'll love her,
If that is what you will.

*Doris.*

    O yes, your love,
Like a small seedling, having little root,
May readily be plucked up from the soil
And planted elsewhere.  Let's to something else:

No more of this.   I had forgot she is your
Pallas-Athene.

*Tremain.*

                    What, an if she be?
Pallas-Athene is not Aphrodite,
And it is Love and Beauty I adore,
Which I find perfect here.  What would you with her?

*Doris.*

She's in my way, was always in my way,
Balked me when we were children, baffled me
In every purpose that I set my heart on,
And brought out all the worst in me, until
He hated me, who should have loved me best.

*Tremain.*

Ah! well; 'tis clear why you should like her ill,
But not so clear how I can meddle.  Would you
That I should carry off a rival beauty,
And leave you a clear field to win your lover,
Breaking my own heart with a frustrate hope?
That is a test of love's unselfishness
Love never claimed before.

*Doris.*

                    And does not now.
The man is nought to me, and never was
Even then before that I had met with you
Who say you love me.

I

*Tremain.*
                    Yet you hint that she
Is in your way.

*Doris.*
                    Well; what if I would be
Revenged upon the gamester who has scorned me,
And she comes in between me and my wrath?
May I not spite him where he most would feel
Cut to the quick?  But there; no more of this.
You'd give your life for me, of course; but when
I ask a trifle, you are scrupulous.
Let it alone.

*Tremain.*
                    What would you have me do?

*Doris.*
Oh, nothing.  I am not so poor in friends
That I must beg of strangers.

*Tremain.*
                    Am I then
Become a stranger to you?  Say, what would you?
I must not hate her—that is not your meaning;
I must not love her—that is less your drift;
But she is in your way—yet not in love's way:
How may I construe this, and do your will?

Am I to tie the offending Beauty, as
In Stamboul, in a sack, and sink her deep
Some evening in the silence and the darkness
Of the mid loch?  Or shall I go in search
Of the lost art of Medicean poison,
And with a kerchief or a pair of gloves,
Subtly envenomed, so assail her life
That straightway she shall pine away and die?
These ways are out of date.  Besides they bring
Vulgar detective fellows, worse than slot-hounds,
About one's heels.

*Doris.*

    Prithee, have done with this:
I might have known that you would trifle with me.
She said you were a coxcomb.

*Tremain.*

       By the heavens,
And all the gods of Hellas, never was
A heart more seriously inclined to serve you
Than mine is, if I only knew the way.

*Doris.*

May I believe you?

*Tremain.*

     Is there any oath
Will carry strong assurance?  I will swear it.

### Doris.

O, yes ; and break it.   Oaths of any kind
Sit easy on the soul that easy takes them :
There is no traitor like your ready swearer
Clothed in the tatters of forgotten vows.

### Tremain.

Nay, I will keep it.   I am in your toils,
And you shall lead me like a meek, tame creature
Whither you will.

### Doris.

   I fancied that a woman,
Having a lover faithful and devoted,
Had but to will, and he would find the way,
His the invention, hers but to desire.—
I've heard indeed of men who with fair speech
Have plied a maiden's heart, and mischief came on't.
But hush ! there's some one coming.

*Enter* FACTOR.

### Factor.

    Good evening, lady.
I am not marring better company ?
May I come in ?

### Doris.

   Yes, certainly.   But what
Brings you again to-day ?

*Factor.*

Well, I have heard
That these Glenara folk will have a grand
Function of their religion there next Sabbath,
A Holy Fair, a big communion-day,
And there will be hot words, they say.

*Doris.*

Can't you
Prevent them?

*Factor.*

That's not easy, if they come
In thousands as their custom is, and get
The drink once in their heads.

*Doris.*

But you can stop
Newspaper men from sending false reports
About the country.

*Factor.*

Yes, yes; I can do
All the reporting they are like to get,
And more than they would wish.  But you might give me
The gillies, and authority from you
To warn them off the ground with threats of law
If they refuse.  They do not like the Law,
Nor does the Law like them.

*Doris.*

   By all means do
Whate'er may stop these dangerous gatherings.

*Factor.*

Thanks; I will see to't. By the way, I met
Your pretty cousin in a pretty plight.

*Doris.*

How mean you? She was here a little ago,
Handsome as ever.

*Factor.*

    Well, she's on the way now
Across the hills, and Kenneth Parlane with her,
Dressed in the rags she wore when she came here,
Barefoot, bareheaded, with her snooded hair,
And the small bundle in the handkerchief
That held her comb, her mother's wedding ring,
Her Bible and Kenneth's letters, prose and verse.

*Doris.*

Oh! she's a fool; and it was like a fool
To think that I could take her from the byre
Into the drawing-room. But let her go.

*Factor.*

I have your full authority, then, to act.

*Doris.*

Surely.   But run no risk of rioting.

*Factor.*

Oh ! never fear.

[*Exit* FACTOR.

*Doris.*

And now you would not mind
Walking across the hill, perhaps, on Sunday?
You'll have rare fun, and you could serve me too.
I have been moving some of my poor tenants
From wretched crofts to settle by the sea,
Where they can fish, and better their estate,
And better, too, my rents by foresting
Their ill-tilled, scanty fields.   They do not like it,
And I would fain know what is said and done
About it at this preaching.   The factor will
Report, of course, but your account would be
More picturesque—perhaps a trifle truer.

*Tremain.*

Certainly, I will go.

*Doris.*

Till then, adieu.
You will think over what I said to you?

### CHORUS.

Cat-like, purring and mewling, and softest rubbing
 of fur,
With just a pat of the claw, now and then, for a
 needed spur,
Touching the quick of his vanity, making him keen
 to go
Whithersoever she would, though whither he did
 not know,
Seeming to answer love with love, though her heart
 was cool,
And the clear-working brain was practising as on a
 fool,
So she played with her victim who thought he was
 playing with her,
For there was not a heart between them to master
 or minister.
Clever the fool might be, yet would she wind him
 around her thumb,
Reason soon to be blinded, conscience soon to be
 dumb ;
For when a woman is good, she doth to all good
 inspire,
But being evil, alas ! she burns up the soul like
 fire.

Rouse thee, man, for an effort; what though her
    speech be smooth,
What though she smile too upon thee in splendour
    of beauty and youth,
There is no pity in her; look at her hard, cold eye;
You she will use for her tool now, and mock with
    her scorn by and by.


## ACT THIRD.—SCENE SECOND.

### CHORUS.

Our fates are linked together, high and low,
    Like ravelled, knotted thrums of various thread,
    Homespun and silk, yellow and green and red,
And no one is alone, nor do we know
From what mean sources great events may flow:
    The tramp that lays him down among the straw,
    Despised, perchance shall fill your home with awe,
Plague-stricken, or from him its peace may grow;
The ruined peasant's cot may downward draw
    The stately hall that neighbours it.  We are
All members of one body, and a flaw
    Or lesion here, the perfect whole shall mar.
Therefore let justice rule, and love inspire;
Wise for thyself, the weal of all desire.

SCENE—The Manse. INA and MORAG.

Morag.

Please, Ina, may I have your leave to go
Away for these two days?

Ina.

Yes, surely, go;

I shall do nicely.

Morag.

That is very well.

Ina.

You do not seem to think so. "Very well"
Sounds e'en like very bad, so drily spoken.

Morag.

If you are happy, it is very well.

Ina.

Indeed I am.

Morag.

But it is sudden—yes !

Yet maybe it will last.

Ina.

Oh, never fear;

'Twill last at any rate till you come back.
I have my books, my music, and to-morrow
There is the church. Of course I'll miss you, yet
I promise to be blithe as any bird.

### Morag.

Oh! very well.

### Ina.

      What ails you, Morag? Would you
Rather that I should sit me down and mope?
You scolded me of late for being sad;
Are you displeased to see me cheerful now,
Blaming alike the sunshine and the cloud?

### Morag.

I see the gulls and pellocks in the loch
Busy and merry, and all the boats are out
Letting the nets down, and the wives are watching
Upon the shore, and talking loud with glee:
And why? Because they see the herring come
Poppling the shining water with their fins,
As if a shower were driving up, although
The sky is blue and clear.

### Ina.

      I'm glad of that;
The poor will now have bread; it is good news.
But what has that to do with it?

### Morag.

      They have
A reason for their happiness.

#### *Ina.*

> O that's it;
You want to know the reason now of mine.
But, Morag, girls are not so rational
As gulls and pellocks.  Have you never felt
Inexplicable sadness overcome you,
Though earth and heaven and all around you were
Filled full of light and song?  Why should not
> joy too
Come whence you cannot tell, nor for what reason,
But just that wells are springing in your heart,
Whose waters lapse, and ripple as they lapse?

#### *Morag.*

Yes, maybe.  Only you were changed that day
You visited Isle-Monach and his grave;
And was it there you found the well of gladness?

#### *Ina.*

You are too curious, prying into what
Concerns you not.  Enough.  There; you may go.
I do not ask you why you wish to go,
Or where you mean to go.

#### *Morag.*

> You ought to ask, then.
A mistress should not let her servants wander
Like hens or ducks at large.

### *Ina.*

      Nor servants let
Their mistress go her own way without giving
Full explanation.  Is it not so, Morag?
But whether I am mistress here or you—
Which may be doubtful—I can wholly trust you.


### *Morag.*

Ina, there was a time when you would take
An interest in us all, and all our doings,
Our comings and our goings and our folk,
The crofters and the cottars and the fishers,
For they belonged to you, and you to them,
Parts of a common life, you said.


### *Ina.*

        Ay, then
I was a fool, and thought to shape your lives,
Who could not guide my own, like some poor
   trader
Who, being bankrupt in his own estate,
Is fain to take the helm, and guide affairs
For all the country.  Do you wish to tell me
About your journey?  I've no right to ask,
Yet less right not to hear you.

*Morag.*

                            But you should
Know all your servants' doings, for it spoils them
Unless they have authority on them;
And better a bad mistress in a house
Than let the maids go gadding as they will.—
But for this business calling me away,
Do you not know, Miss, that to-morrow is
The great Communion at Glenaradale,
And all the country will be there, and half
The godly ministers of Ross and Skye?
O it will be a great time.


*Ina.*

                        Well, I hope
You will enjoy it, Morag.


*Morag.*

                        No, I do not
Know that I will enjoy it.  You enjoy
The bread you eat yourself, but not the bread
That others eat, and which is not for you :
The hungry is not happy when he sees
A sumptuous table spread, and he outside.
I do not hope to enjoy; yet I may get
Share of the crumbs that fall for dogs to eat.

Ina.

O I forgot.  My father always thought,
Morag, that you were wrong there, keeping back
From that which yet you hungered for.

Morag.

It's likely

That he knows better now, and would not be
So loose, if he came back again from heaven,
As then when he came from the lowland folk
Whose kirk is like a market, free to all.

Ina.

That suits me best; I think I dare not go
Except where all alike are free to go.

Morag.

Well, you are free, and it would do you good
To hear the sound of Psalms among the hills
When many thousand voices join, and yet
'Tis like a small child's cry unto the heavens,
Or tinkling of a little brook.

Ina.

I know;

That must be fine indeed.

Morag.

And then the preacher

Tells the glad tiding to the poor; at first,
Just like an auction at a country fair,

Offering his ware so high that none may bid
For that whose price is costlier than rubies;
But in the end the treasure which no wealth
Of man could buy is proffered without money
And without price.

*Ina.*

That's as it ought to be:
But I shall hear the same free Gospel here
From him who soon will be our pastor.

*Morag.*

Him!
It's a thin gospel that you'll get from him.
I bought a pencil one day from the packman,
And I was fain to put a fine point on it,
But ever as I cut, the lead would break,
Just when I had it nearly right; and so
I went on whittling, and it broke and broke,
Till there was nought left but a bit of stick,
And it was sharp enough.  Belike, yon lad
Is whittling down his faith too, like my pencil,
To make a fine point on it, till it be
Only a stump of wood.  Then he must read too
His sermons from a paper!  Och! to think
Of having music-notes for collie dogs
To bark at sheep with!  But the faithful dog
Can do without a paper.  If you heard
Black Eachan of Lochbroom!

*Ina.*

And what of him?

*Morag.*

He's called "The Searcher"; he has no fine points;
But well he knows the doubling and deceit
Of hearts that are like foxes for their wiles;
And does not pore upon a paper, fearful
To lose his place, but has his eye on you
Always, and follows up your very thoughts
Into their holes and secret hiding places,
And hunts you from all coverts, till you lie
Low at his feet, and feel that you are lost.

*Ina.*

I do not envy him.   Why should he drive
Folk to despair?

*Morag.*

He says that to despair
Is to have one foot on the threshold, and
Your finger on the latch.   'Tis very good
For sinners to despair a while.

*Ina.*

My father
Sought to bring hope and comfort to them.

*Morag.*

Yes!
And there was no great work here in his day.

*Ina.*

But there was some good work.  At any rate
I care not for your "Searcher."

*Morag.*
But when he
Has done with you, and you are groaning, maybe,
Over your sins, then Lachlan of the Lews—
"The Trumpet of the Gael"—will take you up,
And like a prophet speak the word of power,
That stirs the desperate heart.  He does not water
The gospel with book-learning; he lets God
Speak for himself in texts and promises,
Like the great word that said to Lazarus,
"Come forth," and he arose.

*Ina.*
If there were prophet
Could move one so!  But no, it cannot be.
'Tis vain to hope for the old faith again
That shone about our childhood.

*Morag.*
Do not doubt
But one of them would have a word for you.

For after these comes Neil of Raasay, maybe;
He has a pleasant voice, as if he played
Sweetly upon an instrument, to tell
About the golden streets, and gates of pearl,
And walls of emerald and amethyst
And topaz, and the river and tree of life,
As if the birds of God had left its boughs,
And come to earth to sing about their glory.

### Ina.

Why, Morag, you are grown poetical
O'er Neil of Raasay.  Yet you did, not seem
To care much for him, when he came at times
To help my father here.

### Morag.

                   He never seemed
Himself when he came here.  Your father was
Too critical, with commentary books
That suck the marrow from the bones of truth,
And leave them dry.  And in a pibroch you
Must have the muster first, and then the fight,
And then the wail, and then the song of triumph:
Nor shall you understand the several parts
Without the others: so it is with him;
You must have Eachan first, and Lachlan next,
And then your heart will glow to Neil of Raasay.

*Ina.*

May be; and yet I think I'll stay at home.
I am not in the mood for strong excitements:
You'll tell me all about it.

*Morag.*

Yes, I'll bring
A true account home of the last great Feast
Held in Glenaradale.

*Ina.*

Nay, not the last.
They have been there a century at least,
And may hold on another, if there's faith
Still in the land, or maybe if there's none:
Such customs linger when the life is gone.

*Morag.*

Have you not heard?  The country's ringing with it.

*Ina.*

Ringing with what?  What is there next to hear?

*Morag.*

Only that Doris has evicted all
The people from their houses, which even now
Are empty, bare, and roofless.  She would crowd them
Upon the strip of shore already thronged
With fishers, and they mean to go away.

They have been used to delve, and handle sheep
And cattle, and they have no skill with boats;
And now they are just waiting for to-morrow,
Housed on the beach, or in the birken wood,
With breaking hearts, before they leave the land.

### *Ina.*

What say you?  Doris root them from the soil
Where they have grown like native heáth or bracken !
And they her kinsfolk !

### *Morag.*

       Ay, but near of kin
May be too near in place for upstart pride.
I've heard some say we are all sprung from apes,
And maybe that's the reason they disgust us
More than a dog or cat.  At any rate,
Glenara is a desert now for deer.

### *Ina.*

Cruel and heartless ! and yet only like her.
Why told you not this story to me first,
Instead of maundering on about the preachings?
What care I for your " Searchers " and your " Trum-
    pets,"
And old Neil Raasay droning about heaven
After his whisky?  But these crofter folk
In green Glenaradale—they touch my heart.

Yes, I will go with you; I will get ready
I' the instant: they shall know they have one friend
Who shares their grief and wrath.

*Morag.*

            But, Ina, think;
It is a twenty miles across the hills
Through moor and moss.

*Ina.*

         And if it be so, think you
I could not do't like other Highland girls
In such a cause?  They fought for Charlie once,
Misled by a belated sentiment,
And by their trust in those who should have wisely
Led them, and only brought them into sorrow:
But who will fight for them now? were I only
A man, at least I'd let my voice be heard
For their poor right of living on the land.

*Morag.*

No, Ina, no; it must not be.

*Ina.*

           What must not?
I may go to the preaching if I will,
But not to visit the oppressed and poor!
That's not it?  O, it is the twenty miles?

Well, I could do it, for my heart is high,
And on the moors among the springy turf
One does not weary as on dusty roads.
But there's no need of walking.  How's the wind?
My boat will bring us cleverly along
To Kinloch-Aradale, within a mile
Of Corrie-an-Liadh.  We shall do it nicely.
O Morag, only think of the old men
With their long memories clinging to the soil,
And babes and mothers on that homeless shore !
I would not bear their curses for the wealth
Of all the world.

*Morag.*

   They will not curse.  But it
Is true, you say; the wind is fair; the boat
Will bear us bravely to Glenaradale.

CHORUS.

Trimly speeds the dainty boat
 Swinging o'er the foam-tipped billow,
Where the keen-eyed sea-mews float
 Sleeping on their watery pillow,
Past the low black Cormorant's Rock,
 Where they crowd in hungry numbers;
There a great grey heron woke,
 Sudden, from its noon-day slumbers,

And beyond, the thrashers rose
　High above where the whale had sickened,
Well could you hear their crashing blows,
　As its labouring breath was quickened:
Till rounding the red headland now,
　The boat leapt out in the open sea,
With a ripple of laughter at her prow,
　And a rush of bubbles upon her lea.

The wind fell low as the sun went down,
And every cloud had a golden crown,
A jewelled belt, and a crimson gown;

And every corrie, and rock, and hill,
Was veiled in pink or in purple, till
The glory was quenched in the gloaming still.

It was the dusk of a sultry night
When Kinloch-Aradale rose in sight,
And on the beach there were fires alight—

Fires alight, and to and fro
Forms among them moving slow,
And on the breeze was a wailing low.

KENNETH'S SONG.

There is no fire of the crackling boughs
On the hearth of our fathers,
There is no lowing of brown-eyed cows
On the green meadows,
Nor do the maidens whisper vows
In the still gloaming,
Glenaradale.

There is no bleating of sheep on the hill
Where the mists linger,
There is no sound of the low hand-mill
Ground by the women,
And the smith's hammer is lying still,
By the brown anvil,
Glenaradale.

Ah ! we must leave thee, and go away
Far from Ben Luibh,
Far from the graves where we hoped to lay
Our bones with our fathers,
Far from the kirk where we used to pray
Lowly together,
Glenaradale.

We are not going for hunger of wealth,
 For the gold and silver,
We are not going to seek for health
 On the flat prairies,
Nor yet for the lack of fruitful tilth
 On thy green pastures,
  Glenaradale.


Content with the croft and the hill were we,
 As all our fathers,
Content with the fish in the lake to be
 Carefully netted,
And garments spun of the wool from thee,
 O black-faced wether
  Of Glenaradale.


No father here but would give a son
 For the old country,
And his mother the sword would have girded on
 To fight her battles;
Many's the battle that has been won
 By the brave tartans,
  Glenaradale.

But the big-horned stag and his hinds, we know,
In the high corries,
And the salmon that swirls the pool below
Where the stream rushes,
Are more than the hearts of men, and so
We leave thy green valley,
Glenaradale.


## ACT THIRD.—SCENE THIRD.

### CHORUS.

Near to the stormy loch, behind
The ridge of the Badger's Rock, there lay
A high green corrie; and there the wind
Was hardly felt on a wild March day,
It was so girdled with hill and rock
That rarely a storm on its stillness broke.
Only the wild deer make their lair
Among the moss and the bracken there,
Or the stealthy fox, or the gled and kite,
Or blue hare and ptarmigan on the height.
Slowly the mountain shadows creep
Across the hollow, across the brook;

And to the right in the rugged steep
　Is a narrow gap where you can look
Right down on the glimmering loch that clings
To the roots of The Hill of a Hundred Springs.

But it is not the red deer that haunt to-day
Corrie-an-Liadh, and crowd the brae,
Here in groups, and there in tiers,
　Till hardly a patch of stone or heather,
　Hardly a green bracken leaf like a feather,
Through the close-packed ranks of the throng appears.
It is men and women, the young and the old,
Some with their snowy locks, some their gold,
Matron or maiden, with cap or snood,
And stalwart sire with his strong-limbed brood—
Men of Glenara with heads bowed low,
Men of Loch Thorar with hearts aglow,
Men of Glen Turret, Glen Shelloch, Glen Shiel,
And lads from the Isles which the mists conceal.

Right at the mouth of that mountain bay
　There is a mound of swelling green
Whereon the golden sunbeams play,
　And daisy and pansy flowers are seen,
And close beside it a trickling spring
Circled with moss and draped with ling.

There once they offered sacrifice,
  Bringing their sick to the healing well,
And the kid of a goat for a ransom price
  To the Spirit that bound and loosed the spell;
There now a table is seemly spread
  With homely linen, but clean and white,
And a chalice and platter with wheaten bread,
  And the Book that giveth the blind their sight;
And the sun shines down, who had seen before
Far other rites in the days of yore.

Pastors four on the swelling mound
Sit, rapt, as if upon holy ground—
One with a great black shock of hair,
One with a smiling face and fair,
One that was pale, and lean, and young,
With a fire in his heart and a flame on his tongue,
One the old pastor of the Gael
Driven out of green Glenaradale,
With grey locks streaming around a face
That beamed with a light of tender grace.
Another group behind them lay
  Stretched, careless, out on the short hill grass;
They were not there to praise or pray,
  But jest and gibe they were fain to pass,
And kept apart from all the rest,

And not in Sabbath raiment drest;—
The factor, with gillies, and dogs, and whips,
And the poet with heathendom on his lips.
They came from walking to and fro
Upon the earth, as long ago
One came with the sons of God, we know.


Scene—*Corrie-an-Liadh. Throng of people seated on bank:*
 Ina, Morag, Kenneth, *and* Mairi *in front of* Factor,
 Tremain, *and others behind the Ministers.*


*A " Man " (passing the Factor).*
Is Saul among the prophets?

       *Factor.*
        Why not, Dugald?
Saul found them singing in the dance, and joined
The sport, of course.

      " *Man.*"
        This is no day for sport.

      *Factor.*
O, that depends: I've known some queer folk now
Whose acid looks would sour the cream on Monday,
Yet make some fun for you with texts on Sunday.

"*Man.*"

You are a flippant person; but your day
Will not be long, though God may wink awhile.

*Factor.*

I'll take my chance.   The wink may grow a nap
As you pray, Dugald.   Few can stand that long.

"*Man.*"

Blasphemer !                              [*Passes on to his seat.*

*Factor.*

Hypocrite !

*Tremain.*

                            Nay, hold your peace;
I like not these men's looks: they're stern and grim,
And knit their brows in silence, and their knuckles
Are white, see, as they clench their great brown fists.

*Factor.*

Nay, never fear, sir.   Don't I know them well?
The law is powerful; not a man of them
Dare wag his tongue at me.

*Tremain.*

                            They're in the mood
For more than wagging tongues.   And for the law,
What if they have the right on't?

*Factor.*

            Let them break
The peace, and then they will be in the wrong.
I'll keep safe with the law.  Lads, give the dogs
A nip, and set them howling, when you hear
The minister begin to clear his throat.

*Tremain.*

Why do you that?

*Factor.*

           'Twill be as good a joke
As bumming of an organ in their ears,
Or tuning of a fiddle for the psalm.

*Tremain.*

I pray you, stop.  See you not every man
Grasping his staff?  There is a thousand there
For one of us.

*Factor.*

        So be it.  They would tell you
" The Lord can work by many or by few."
You do not fear that rabble?

*Tremain.*

            Yes, I do.
Somehow the big battalions always win,
And one may doubt if God is on our side.
Let them alone.

*The people sing, to a Celtic tune,*

"I to the hills will lift mine eyes,
  From whence doth come mine aid.
My safety cometh from the Lord,
  Who heav'n and earth hath made."

*Tremain.*

                         'Tis a pathetic strain
In a barbaric minor long drawn out;
So the Greek chorus might be sung, when they
Played a fate-drama in their sacred feasts.
Hush! stop that yelping.    There will be cracked
    crowns
If this go on.—But what proud pallid face
Is that among them?  O, my stately Beauty,
Pallas-Athene of the waterfall,
And Doris' pet aversion, whom I have
To strangle, drown, or poison—anything
But love.  I think I'll throw me at her feet.
It is a face to dream on; safer there
Than here, too, and the seats are not reserved.
                    [*Crosses to* INA, *and lies down on grass.*

*Factor.*

White-livered fool!  But let him go.  What's this
The minister is after?  Make a speech
Without a text!  Who ever heard the like?
And what's come of the prayer?  Be ready, lads.

*Minister.*

My friends, this is a day of solemn sadness
With us, for we shall ne'er all meet again
Here where our fathers met these hundred years,
Remembering the love of Him who came,
In power of sorrow, to redeem from sorrow,
And sin which is its fountain.   It is not
That sere and withered leaves shall drop in autumn;—
That always will be: nor that tender buds,
Frost-bitten, die untimely in their spring:
Nor that the hale and well may also fall,
Reft by the stormy winds;—all that may be
To any people, and at any time:
To-morrow only knows what it shall bring.
But human law, defying the divine,
Which gave the land for man to dwell therein,
And to replenish and subdue its wildness,
Straining the rights of those who own the soil
By writs and deeds, wherein they gave it over
Who had no property in it to give,
Has torn up by the roots a band of you,
Loyal and dutiful and fearing God
As any in the land; and nevermore
Shall we together sing our psalm of praise here,
Or break the bread, or drink the cup of blessing.
Therefore is this a solemn day with us,

Touched with the sadness of their leave-taking,
And with regretful memories.

*Factor.*

                Take care, sir,
You're on the verge of treasonable speech
Against the law.

*Minister.*

           We do not break the law,
Even when it breaks the hearts that it should bind
Closer to home and country.  Neither would I
Pour Mara water now into the cup
Heaven sweetened with the wood of His dear cross,
Who loved us.  Men may wreck your happy homes,
But God is building better mansions for you.
They make a desert—He a paradise;
They drive you over sea, but He will bring you
Where there is no more sea.  And we should take
The losses and the crosses of our life
As hooks to fasten us to that better world.

*Factor.*

Ay, that is right.  They'll find a better world
In Canada; you hook them on to that.

*Minister.*

Be silent, sir.  I will not speak of her

Whose high imperious order drives you forth,
Homeless——

#### Factor.

Nor will I hear a generous lady,
Who is too good a landlord for such people,
So shamefully abused.  I tell you, sir,
This is mere cant, fanatic and illegal,
Stirring ill blood in those who know no better
By those who should know better.

#### Minister.

Pray you, sir,
Have patience; I have spoken nought amiss;
Do not disturb our worship.

#### Factor.

Worship ! call ye't ?
You preach against the law and call that worship !
Against the landlord, and that's worship too !
I will not hold my peace.  You people, hear !
Go to your homes, or to your parish kirks,
Or it will be the worse for you.  This place
Is not for people to denounce the law,
Or landlords in their legal rights.  The Book
Will have you to obey the Powers that be,
And speak no evil of them.  There is clear
Chapter and verse for that.  A pretty worship !

*Minister.*

Take heed, sir, what you do.   You have no law
For this.

*Factor.*

              Away !  I tell you, or I'll set
The dogs upon you.

*A " Man."*

                    Och ! ochone ! and is
The Lord, too, banished from Glenaradale
To Canada?

*Another " Man."*
              Ochone ! will it be Baal
Or Moloch that the factor will be having
On the high places to pollute the land?

*Another " Man."*
It is a day of darkness and dismay,
A day of wrath for broken covenants,
And for dishonoured Sabbaths.

*Minister.*
                    Sir, I warn you
The people now look dangerous.   Be quiet,
Or leave us : do not drive them mad.

*Factor.*
                              Away !
Ye are trespassers, and I know you well !
I will have writs out on you by to-morrow.

*A " Man."*
Now, who will come with me to help the Lord
Against the factor?

*A Fisherman.*
                    That will I do, Dugald.

*A Crofter.*
Yes, and it iss not you will be alone.
Away with him !  He tore my shieling down,
And Ailie's babe just born.

*Another Crofter.*
                        And he insulted
The minister !  Yes, it iss fery well !
There iss the Tod's Hole yonder, and the Loch
Iss deep below it.
                *Crowd (rushing forward).*
                    To the Tod's Hole with him !
                *Minister.*
Nay, hear me, O my people, I entreat you;
Do not this crime, for Christ's sake.  Will ye not
Listen a moment?  O my God, that men
Should do foul murder !  On the Sabbath, too !

Stay, stay, I tell you.  Heaven have mercy on him,
For they are deaf as adders.

Ina (rising up).

Morag, this
Is frightful.  Kenneth, can you not do aught
To help him?  See, they drag the wretched man
Struggling, entreating, cursing, praying, while
They move in stern grim silence to the gap
In the black rugged rock, that looks right down
Into the Otter's Hole.  [*To* TREMAIN.]  Can you look on, sir,
And see your comrade murdered?  You came with him
To find your sport, and lo ! he finds a death,
Too horrible, instead.

Tremain.

What can I do?
They will not hear the parson plead in Gaelic,
How should they heed me with my English tongue?
Indeed, I tried to stop him, but in vain.
Think you that, if I sung an Orphic song,
Mellifluous, melodious, as e'er
Hushed Philomela, shamed of her sweet strain,
These grim and silent executioners
Of Nature's law would listen?  Truly I would
Do anything, fair lady, for your grace.

And yet, to see your pity and your terror
So tragically moved and beautiful,
I'd almost let him fall from cutting ledge
To jutting crag into the hungry loch.

### *Ina.*

Tush !

### *Morag.*

          Well, this man is madder than a foumart,
He would kill folk to see how one might look.

### *Tremain.*

Nay, not how you would look; there is no grand
Pathetic grace in you.

### *Ina.*

          Now, who is that
Standing upon the sharp edge of the rock
At the Tod's Hole.  Ah ! Diarmid.  All is well.

### *Sir Diarmid.*

Go back, now, lads, and hear the minister;
Vengeance belongs to God.  You would not stain
Your hands with blood from such a puddle as this.

### *A " Man."*

Out of our way, Sir Diarmid; we have no
Quarrel with you, but this man's cup iss full.

### Sir Diarmid.

I will not budge an inch, and you must kill me
Before you break a bone of him; and that
You would be loath to do.  There; you have given
The scamp a fright he will not soon forget;
That's all you meant, and he deserved it well,
Bully and coward!

### Kenneth.

   Yes, the chief is right;
Let him go now.  I'll make a ballad of
His teeth that chattered like a castanet.

### A " Man."

He hass been like an iron flail with teeth
To all the folk, sir; but it iss your will.

### Sir Diarmid.

Yes; ere he go, then, let him have a shake
Such as your terriers give an ugly rat,
And then have done with him.  You would not
  make
This day a day of horror and reproach
For such as cur as that.  So: that is right.
       [*They let him go.*
I do not wonder that your hearts were hot.

### Minister.

Now, God be praised, who brought you here, Sir
    Diarmid.
Ere that was done which never could be undone,
And put the heart in you, and gave you power
Over the people's hearts to move them, like
An instrument of music, at your will.
I marvel not that they were wroth at him;
The man is of an evil nature, hard
And insolent and cruel to the poor,
And servile to the great, and knowing law
Only to strain its power, and make it hateful.

### Tremain (coming up).

There, parson, now your Deus did not come
In a cloud-chariot driven by mighty angels,
But riding on a nag, a simple laird.

### Minister.

Be not profane, sir; and for you, my people,
Ye have been saved from doing greater wrong,
But wrong ye have done; and how shall we sing
The Lord's song, with the swell of that late storm
Still rolling in our hearts?   Let us go back,
And humble us, confessing all the sin.
                   *[Return to their seats.*

*Tremain.*

Diarmid, the factor now will hate you almost
As much as he will hate this pious mob.
You saved his life, 'tis true, but only saved it
By showing him a thing to scorn and loathe;
You should have had more tact.   He'll not forget it.

*Sir Diarmid.*

What care I for his hatred or his love?
But how came you, of all men, to be here
Of all scenes on this earth?

*Tremain.*

                      Why should I not
Enrich my soul with all experiences
Of life and passion, to be moulded duly
Into pure forms of art?   I came to see
The Christian superstition where I heard
The thing was really living.   Up in town
'Tis but a raree-show of surplices
And albs and copes and silver candlesticks
And droning repetitions; poor survivals
Of the old Pagan cult: or else it is
A small dissenting shop where they retail
Long yards of worn-out logic, or an ounce
Of bitter morals, with a syllabub
Of sentiment.   But this is different.

I could have almost fancied I was back
With Cyril in the Alexandrian desert,
And throngs of howling unwashed monks who hunted
A Neo-Platonist: only yon factor
Is no philosopher.

*Sir Diarmid.*

　　　　Came you not with him?

*Tremain.*

Well, yes; he promised I should have some sport;
And there was Doris' tenantry to see to.

*Sir Diarmid.*

Are you so close confederates already?

*Tremain.*

We've but one thought, one aim, one life between us.
And such a life!　She is a glorious galley,
Freighted with gold and gems, and silks and spices,
And all the treasures of the fabled East,
And at a word she struck to me.

*Sir Diarmid.*

　　　　That's well;
You poets are the men to win your way
Into a maiden's heart by flattery.
Now, you must go and see the factor home;
His bones are stiff, I fancy.

*Tremain.*

      Nay, there is
A lady in the crowd—Pallas-Athene—
She sought mine aid, and I must go to her.

*Sir Diarmid.*

Leave her to me; you must see to your friend.
Doris would scarcely care to think you left
Her factor for a stranger damosel.

*Tremain.*

Doris must learn to put up with a heart
That loves all beauty, and has room for all.
I must go back to her.

*Sir Diarmid.*

      Be off, I tell you,
Unless you'd rather I should hurl you down,
'Stead o' the factor, from the Tod's Hole yonder.
         [*Exit* TREMAIN.
The jackanapes! Yet, if he speaks the truth,
I am near happiness. Now for Ina.
         [*Goes towards her.*

*Ina.*

      Diarmid !

*Sir Diarmid.*

Come with me, Ina; let me take you hence;
This scene has been too much for you.

#### Ina.

                                Ah ! yes ;
I know not if your courage, or my fears
Shook me the most.  It was a daring thing
To stand up in the breach, and brave their fury.

#### Sir Diarmid.

Nonsense.   I knew they would not harm a hair
Of my head, more than sheep would fly upon
The dog that herds them;  and you do not call
The collie quite a hero.

#### Ina.

                        Do not leave me,
Diarmid.  I know 'tis silly, but I feel
So weak and trembling.

#### Morag.

                        Ina, you're not going,
Just when they've got all ready for the work
Of this great day.

#### Sir Diarmid.

                        Yes, Morag, she must go.
Do you not see her shaking like a leaf?

#### Morag.

Black Eachan's giving out a psalm.  They'll think
It strange if we should leave now.

#### Sir Diarmid.

          Never mind;
There, Ina, lean on me; my arm is strong,
             *[Move off.*
And my heart lighter than it has been lately,
For there were troubles that did threat our love.

#### Ina.

Yes, I could see that something was amiss,
Something that made you moody and reserved,
Though you were only gentler, dear, with me.

#### Sir Diarmid.

And yet you never asked me what was wrong.

#### Ina.

I knew you would have told me if I ought
To know; and though I longed to share it with
   you
I held my peace till you should speak.  It is not
For love to be too curious, but to trust.

#### Sir Diarmid.

And for that trust I thank you.  More than once
It was upon my tongue to tell you all,
And leave it to your heart—for it is wise—
To say what I should do.  But then I thought
It would be mean to shift my burden off

And lay it upon you.  Now it grows clear,
However, and a day or two will end it.
Trust me till then, and then I'll never leave you,
Till life leaves me.  But there's the boat all trim,
And a brisk breeze will take us swiftly home.


### CHORUS.

O that sail on the summer sea!
  Can she ever forget its gladness?
Yet O the haunting memory
Of those bright hours, when they came to be
  The wistfullest sigh of the day of sadness!

## ACT FOURTH.—SCENE FIRST.

### CHORUS.

Close by a lake, beneath a long-backed hill
 A lodge stood new and bare;
  Larch and spruce had been planted there,
   But they were still
Only like tufts of grass upon the long-backed hill.
   There, by no care oppressed,
   The wanderer now found rest
  Who had seen many cities, many men,
   And many perils known,
   And many a die had thrown
  With risk of all his living now and then.
Skimming the surface lightly and alone
 Gaily he took what pleasure might be got;
No higher life the stirring West had shown,
 The brooding East called forth no deeper thought.

M

Yet could he shrewdly use his wits,
And had his cautious, prudent fits,
His memories also, and regrets
　　That touched his heart with lights from
　　　　heaven,
Though he sat easy under debts
　　Of duty, that had surely driven
To their wits' end respectable good folk
Who went to church, and no commandment broke.


SCENE—*Glen Chroan Lodge.*　DR. LORNE *and* CHUNDRA,
　　　　　　*his servant.*

*Chundra.*

The Begum, sahib!　I have seen her.

*Dr. Lorne.*
　　　　　　　　　　　　　　Tush !
We have no Begums here.

*Chundra.*
　　　　　　　I saw her—her !

*Dr. Lorne.*

Why, man, she has been dead these ten years past,
And more.

*Chundra.*
　　　　Yes, sahib, dead ten years ; and yet
I saw her, and she smiled ; and then I said
What devilry is brewing?

*Dr. Lorne.*
I never knew
Of any ghost that had been ten years dead,
And yet came smiling back.  They lose their smile,
Chundra, exactly in the seventh year,
And it returns no more, because they have not
Lips, cheeks, or eyes to smile with, though the teeth
Grin horribly.  But, now, I'm rather busy;
I'll hear you by and by.  I am expecting
A visitor on matters of grave moment:
You'll show him in, and see that no one enters
While he is here.  Have tiffin ready, too,
On the instant notice, mind.

*Chundra.*
Yes, Doctor sahib.
[*Exit Servant.*

*Dr. Lorne.*
I partly guess what Begum he has seen;
She's like her mother, doubtless.  Well, I've got
A pill to purge her devilry, if she
Is at the old one's tricks.

*Chundra.*
Sir Bennett, sahib.
*Enter* BENNETT.

### Dr. Lorne.

Good morning, Bennett.   Had a pleasant journey?

### Bennett.

So so; your nags are good enough, but then
Your roads are something perpendicular,
And what with ruts and rocks they make hard
       driving.

### Dr. Lorne.

There; how you lawyers grumble!  If you knew
The roads I've gone by dâk!  And for your climb,
You got the better view of scenery
Thought to be well worth seeing.  But now, Bennett,
Our Highland air is reckoned hungry air;
Shall you bait first, or work?

### Bennett.

                    Let us to business;
It spoils alike the dinner and digestion
To have work hanging o'er you, like the skull
At the old feasts.

### Dr. Lorne.

                 So be it, then; and yet
I fear your patience may be tried beyond
Endurance of your appetite.  You know
Old travellers claim the right to be long-winded.

*Bennett.*

I can recruit me at the sideboard there,
If you abuse your privilege.

*Dr. Lorne.*

All right.

And so now to my tale.  You knew my brother,
The Parson, Ronald; we were twins, alike
In form and feature, but in mind—— Ah! well;
He was the family saint, and I the pickle,
From childhood.  So he took to healing souls,
And I to doctoring people's pains and aches
And indigestions—he for love of souls,
And I for love of fees.  I did my work,
As others did, by rule; went feeling pulses,
Looking at tongues, and writing out prescriptions
With a good conscience, and a look of wisdom.
I knew the dose was dropt into the dark,
But it was what our high tradition ordered.
Sometimes it cured, but how, I could not tell;
Sometimes it failed, and why I did not know:
God orders all; except He build the house
They labour in vain that build it.  So I took
My fee, and silently allowed the *vis*
*Naturæ medicatrix*, and the *mors*
That beats with equal foot at every door.

*Bennett.*

Quite right; what other could you do?


*Dr. Lorne.*

                                        Even so
It seemed.   And yet, if Nature worked the cure,
Nature should have the fee too; and besides
My conscience got entangled with new science
That would have no empiric, no hap-hazard;
And I must go but where it showed the way—
And O, it had so little way to show:
So I lost faith in all our Therapeutic.


*Bennett.*

Queer, now: I had a parson with me lately
Wanting to strip his gown off.  He had dropt,
Bit by bit, all old formulas of faith,
And buried all his gods, he said, and saw
No difference in his flock who came to church,
And said their prayers, and hardly pricked their ears
At any fresh negation; traded, feasted,
And gossipped as before—nor worse nor better,
A moral class of pure respectables.
But he opined his life would be a lie
If he went on.

*Dr. Lorne.*
And surely so it had been.
What counsel gave you him?


*Bennett.*
                        Bade him go home,
And write his sermon, said I envied him
Having so clear a case, so plain a brief,
Authority so full, and absolute law
To preach the gospel.   But the fellow went
And took to writing novels—he is lost.
Yet it is odd that ministers and doctors
Should be so sceptic in their own affairs:
You'll never find a lawyer acting so.
I have my doubts, like other folk, but keep them
Clear of my business.


*Dr. Lorne.*
          Some have doubts of it.


*Bennett.*
Ay, but they're laymen.


*Dr. Lorne.*
                    Lucky you that can
Doubt every thing, except that law is right,

And bide unmoved when all around is shifting.—
But to my story: like your parson, I
Flung up my craft, but did not take to writing,
Having no knack that way; and though I had
No faith in physic, I had faith enough
In my own luck.  Therefore I went abroad,
And drifted round the world, now up, now down,
Making a fortune one day, losing it
Another, now in rags among the miners,
Then swaggering from a "hell" where the croupiers
Hated the sight of me.  A pretty game
Life is now, if you only have the pluck
To brave the worst it can do.

*Bennett.*

> Maybe so;
But how about your conscience now, that scrupled
At physic?   Could it swallow dice and cards?

*Dr. Lorne.*

Quite readily: I take it that a conscience
Is like an Arab horse that frets and fidgets
In the strait streets where people congregate;
But let it free i' the wilds, and it obeys
The lightest touch.  At last I found myself—
After a run of luck in India—
Up in a native state—netting one day
Some hundred thousand, odds.

*Bennett.*

Then you came home
To your snug place here.

*Dr. Lorne.*

Not a bit of it.
I said, "Now, if I keep this, ten to one
'Twill vanish at the next turn o' the wheel;
And yet I cannot give the game up yet,
Or settle down, respectable, to grow
Fungi and mosses on my brains at home.
But there's my brother, dear old fellow, starving
In the old manse, where we all starved in youth,
I'll send it him, and he will use it well."

*Bennett.*

The whole of it?

*Dr. Lorne.*

Well, pretty nearly so.
I kept a nest-egg, or I scarce had been
Where I am now. But listen; I am coming
Straight to the point at last. I knew poor Ronald
Would never take it as a gift from me,
Would only bank it in my name—he had
No notion of investing even—and so
If things went wrong, as they had often done,
Why, it would go, as other gains had gone,
To hungry creditors.

*Bennett.*

I see.  But how
Avoid that, if he would not take your gift?

*Dr. Lorne.*

That's what I had to settle.  Well, there was
A crofter fellow from Glenaradale,
Who had gone partners with me in some ventures,—
Railway-contracting, money-lending, what not?
I took him for my friend, for I had done him
A good turn more than once.  This man I made
My banker; giving it in charge to him
To send the money to my brother here,
When he next heard of me, which should be soon.

*Bennett.*

But you took vouchers?

*Dr. Lorne.*

Surely; here they are;
And that is why I sent for you, to know
If they be valid, as I think they are.
He dealt in money, managed our exchanges,
Contracted, too, for railways; a smart fellow,
Jobbing at everything, and everything
Brought money to him—so they said at least.
But to my plot.  Having set all this right,
As I supposed, I went and drowned myself.

*Bennett.*

Drowned yourself!   Well, you take your drowning
  kindly.

*Dr. Lorne.*

Next day there was a body—a white man's
From the up-country somewhere—floated down
The river with a pocket-book of mine
Found on him, where they did not know my face.
I read the notices of my decease
In the newspapers, one day, in Japan,
Months afterwards.   They gave me on the whole
A character for enterprise and honour,
My brother read at home with grateful tears,
And I in Tokyo with mirth and laughter.

*Bennett.*

What could you mean by such a foolish trick?
How could this drowning help you?

*Dr. Lorne.*

Don't you see?
To take a gift of eighty thousand pounds
Was one thing to a kind of thin-skinned conscience,
And quite another thing a legacy
From his dead brother lying in his grave.

*Bennett.*

Well, well; you're a mad fellow.   But the money—

*Dr. Lorne.*

Was never heard of more.   My clever friend
Had married in the native state a woman
We used to call the Begum—a volcano
Incarnate, an embodied thunder-bolt,
Fat, greedy, false, and cunning as a serpent,
And yet a fierce tornado.   I've no doubt
She set him on to write that I had died
In debt, and hunted up some old accounts
Which the poor parson paid.   They were but trifles,
Yet he would wear a shabbier coat for them.
I almost could forgive the theft, but not
That dirty trick on him, the scurvy rogue!

*Bennett.*

Ah! your too clever schemes miscarry always.
But what came of your Begum?

*Dr. Lorne.*

                              O she died
Ten years ago; and Cattanach came home
With a fine half-breed daughter, and my money,
Which bought Glenaradale: and then he died.

*Bennett.*

The papers now? But did you never write
Your brother?

*Dr. Lorne.*

     No; he thought that I was dead;
And I thought oft, when things were tight with me,
What plenty there would be in the old manse,
And that somehow contented me.

*Bennett.*

          The vouchers?

*Dr. Lorne.*

Well, here they are; it was a native lawyer
Drew them up for me, but I think they're right.

*Bennett.*

Leave me alone a while;—at least be quiet,
Unless I ask a question. 'Tis a case
Needs an old lawyer's skill. Of course he held
That you were dead indeed, and the temptation
Was too much for him. Opportunity
Makes rogues as heat breeds worms in carrion;
You gave him just the chance to turn a rascal.
A most mad business! Had you but consulted
A lawyer, now, you might have had your will,
And he might have been honest to this day.

*Dr. Lorne.*

Nay, but he was a rogue in grain, I fear,
And never took the straight road, when a crooked
Came handy to him.

*Bennett (reading).*

   Right, right; clear as day.
Not a flaw in them.  Who could have believed
A yellow Hindoo could have made a case
So tight as this?   There's only one thing now.
How about that same drowning in the river?

*Dr. Lorne.*

Read on.

*Bennett.*

  I see.  Compeared before the Judge;
Witnesses certify that you are you,
And that the dead man was not you.  All right.
And now, sir, we may dine with easy minds.

*Dr. Lorne.*

Then we can do it?

*Bennett.*

  Do it! we can wring
Both principal and interest from his heirs
To the last mite.  I have not time to sum it,

But it will take a many Highland acres
Of hill and moor to clear it; and there's nothing
Will clear his character.

*Dr. Lorne.*

                He had none to lose.
Then you will take the case in hand for me?

*Bennett.*

Will I consent to eat your venison,
Pick well-kept grouse, and drink your dry champagne,
Or orderly draw up a long account
For a good client?  Will I consent, quotha?
Why, if the case were only half a case,
Instead of what it is, a certainty,
There is no lawyer could refuse so neat
Compact a job.  It's really beautiful.

*Dr. Lorne.*

Then we shall go and dine.

*Bennett.*

                  By all means dine.
I never felt both appetite and conscience
So sweetly go together.  If you have
A bottle of old port, you're safe to draw it;
'Twill not be wasted on me.

### CHORUS.

So they sit there and drink
   Port, crusted, that mellows
   Even crusty old fellows
That are well on the brink
   Of the threescore and ten
   Appointed for men
To labour and think,
And to eat here and drink.
O the night that they spent!
   And the stories they told!
And the bottles that went
   Like shorn sheep to the fold!
What did the ordered household say?
And what could the old men think next day?


## ACT FOURTH.—SCENE SECOND.


### CHORUS.

When frank, straight-forward hearts defile
Their ways with some unwonted wile
   And crafty stroke,
In their own gin they are ensnared,

And better they had onward fared
        With simple folk :
        The choicest and wisest
            Of all the world is he
        Who talks still, and walks still
            In clear sincerity.

Let moles work underground, and mine,
Let adders creep with supple spine
            Through grass and ling,
Let pee-wits lure you from their nest
With wailing cry, and drooping crest,
            And broken wing :
        But you, man, be true, man,
            And, artless, jog along
        The highways ; for byeways
            Will surely lead you wrong.

SCENE—*Cairn-Cailleach.*   DORIS *and* FACTOR DUFFUS.

### *Doris.*

There, Duffus, never mind : you're not much hurt,
And they shall pay for this.

### *Factor.*

                        My bones are whole,
But all my joints are aching, and my feelings
Cruelly wounded.   Does that count for nothing?

#### *Doris.*

Well, well; we'll find a plaster soon to heal
Your wounded feelings: we'll have law on them.
You say Sir Diarmid took their part?

#### *Factor.*

                       He did;
Mocked me, insulted me, called me a rat
For dogs to worry, bade them shake me well
As terriers might.  He seemed to save my life,
But I believe 'twas all arranged before.

#### *Doris.*

And Ina Lorne was there too?

#### *Factor.*

                    Yes; I saw her
Stand up and wave her hands, as hounding on
Their murderous fury.

#### *Doris.*

              Enter your complaint then;
Get the ringleaders clapt in jail.  The sheriff
Will not be slack in dealing with those "Men"
Who mar our mirth and music.

#### *Factor.*

               Yes; perhaps
They might be brought before the higher court,

If we went warily about it.   Some
Have even been hanged for less.

#### Doris.

         I daresay.   Well ;
At any rate we'll make them rue this job,
Gentle and simple of them.   Now, good-bye ;
Drive to the town and get your warrants out.

#### Factor.

I'll lose no time.
             [*Exit* FACTOR.

#### Doris.

         A letter from Sir Diarmid,
Formal and stiff, asking an interview.
What does it mean?   It cannot be this riot,
And threatening of the factor's life ; that is
Too trifling, though I'll make them suffer for it.
It looks like business, and yet our affair
Had never less of promise, as I think.
What can it be.   He is too much a man
To beg remission of his debt.   What then?
Can he have dreamed that I have given my heart
To that word-monger who would buy my wares
With promises to pay, and no effects
To meet his promise?   Well, if that's his game,—
As I half think it is, being so shallow,

And like a man's dull wits—if he will ask me
In the fond hope that I will now refuse,
Being love-pledged to yonder popinjay,—
O the flat fool!—Do I then love him truly?
I hardly know; it might have been so once,
Had he once truly sought my love; but this
I'm sure of, that I hate with all my soul
The girl that robbed me of him.  Could I break
Her heart now, though I wrecked my life on it,
Would I not do it?  Once I thought to send
That popinjay to her, in hopes that he
Might babble a love tale into her ear,
And make her public by a wicked poem :
Or false or true, it matters not.  But that
Had been a bootless errand; for she moves
Like some clear star in the serenities,
So far beyond his reach he could not smirch her
Even by his praise.  But there.  The hour is near,
And I must smooth the ruffles from my face,
Try to look sweet and innocent, and yet
Keep my head clear.  I may need all my wits.

*Enter* SIR DIARMID.

*Sir Diarmid.*

Good morning, Doris !  You are looking radiant :
I need not ask, How do you?

### *Doris.*

                    Well, of course;
That question is a superfluity
Of custom, at a loss what else to say.
But now I think on't, is there aught ails you?
You scarce reflect the radiance you are pleased
To see in me.

### *Sir Diarmid.*

                    O, I am always strong
And healthy as a ploughman.  But we men
Have cares of business on us; and besides,
Our faces never have the light of yours;
They are horn-lanterns, and their light is dim,
Fit only for the stable.

### *Doris.*

                    Oh!  But, Diarmid,
I never knew you were so greatly bent
On business.  Yet I'm glad : it's like a man.
Boys only think of shooting, fishing, sport,
And girls of balls and dresses.  But a man—
You see how wise I grow—takes up his task
Of duty bravely, or sadly at the worst.
This will delight your mother.

*Sir Diarmid.*

Nay, I know not
That I'm so fond of work, or that my mother
Has any reason to be proud of me.
But, like or not like, one has work to do,
And trouble with it, and the less you like it
The more it troubles you

*Doris.*

O, but you ought
To like it, Diarmid.  If you only saw
How sharply I look after my affairs,
And knit my brows o'er long accounts, and make
My lips like wafers, doing dreadful sums!
And when they're done I jump right up, and sing,
Or waltz about the room.

*Sir  Diarmid.*

Well; my affairs
Will hardly set me waltzing as I look
Into them closely.  It is well that yours
Leave you so light of heart.

*Doris.*

Why, what is wrong?—
O, by the way, my factor has been here;
Poor man! his bones are full of aches and bruises,

And he complains of you that you encouraged
Those rascals of Glenaradale to worry
His life nigh out of him.  I hardly thought
That you would aid the rabble in their outbreaks
Against their natural leaders.

### *Sir Diarmid.*

                              He abused
Your ears in saying this.  I saved his life;
And that's his gratitude !

### *Doris.*

                         Well, I only heard
His side, of course.  I hope your case is clear;
He has gone to the fiscal to complain.

### *Sir Diarmid.*

E'en let him go : he'll not make much of that.
And, Doris, when the truth comes out of this
Same natural leadership which never leads,
And cares not for the flock but for the fleece,
It will provoke sharp comment.  In these days,
We live beneath the eye and surveillance
Of all the world, and public sentiment
Is not with us, let Law say what it will,
For we have made it in our interests.

### Doris.

Will public sentiment—whate'er that be,
And I suppose it's just newspaper babble—
Back up a threat of murder, and a brutal
Assault on one who simply did his duty?

### Sir Diarmid.

No, surely.　But was Duffus in the line
Of duty, jeering at the poor folk's worship,
Setting his dogs a-howling to their psalms,
And ordering them to leave the hallowed place,
So linked with their most sacred thoughts and
　　feelings,
Where they had met these hundred years?

### Doris.

　　　　　　　　　　　Of course,
You have been hearing Ina Lorne.　She'll find
Herself in trouble some day.

### Sir Diarmid.

　　　　　　　　　　Be it so :
I'd rather stand with those poor men, and bear
The sentence of the Law, than feel the verdict
O' the general conscience cover me with scorn.—
But it was not my errand to discuss
These matters with you.

*Doris.*

What then was the business
That brought you?

*Sir Diarmid.*

It is kind in you to give me
This meeting, though I fear I am too late.

*Doris.*

Nay, you were punctual to a minute, Diarmid.
I've noticed that you have that excellent habit
Of business.

*Sir Diarmid.*

What I meant was, that my errand
Might be too late, forestalled perhaps, and useless.

*Doris.*

What is your errand then?  I cannot think
What matter there could be between us two
To make you stammer so, and hesitate.

*Sir Diarmid.*

Idle enough, if I may judge from all
I see and hear; and I confess my claims
Are weak compared to his, for he can give you
A name among the brilliant company
Of wits and scholars in the capital,

Who rightly could appreciate your rare beauty,
And your fine gifts of mind.  Well; must I then
Congratulate you, Doris, or go on?

*Doris.*

I do not understand you; but go on,
If there be anything to go on to.

*Sir Diarmid.*

Pardon me.  I had heard my friend had won
Your love, as well he merits.  He said as much.

*Doris.*

Who gets his merits?  Some folk think themselves
Worth all the world, while all the world thinks them
Too slight to be accounted of.  Your friend,
Was he then boasting of a conquest?

*Sir Diarmid.*

　　　　　　　　　　　　　　　　Nay;
Not boasting, only glad, as well he might be,
To win so fair a prize.  And my small merit
Is nothing beside his, nor could it gain,
I fear, by my poor telling.  It did not
Astonish me that one so brilliant plucked
The fruit from me.

*Doris.*

Was this your errand then,
To know if I am plighted to your friend
Whom I'll not name, as you do name him not?
I thought such questions commonly were left
To curious women.

*Sir Diarmid.*

That was not my errand :
But that, if it were true, would make my errand
A useless one, which need not trouble you.

*Doris.*

Better to say out what you meant to say
About yourself, than question me of love
Which, till it choose to speak, should scarce be asked
asked
To break its silence.

*Sir Diarmid.*

Well, I did not come
To speak of love, though love should be the theme
Of such discourse. But truth is more than all ;
And that you have a right to get.

*Doris.*

Please don't ;
It sounds so dreadful serious. There is always

Something unpleasant in the wind, when people
Tell you they'll speak the truth.  In school-girl days
'Twas always the preamble of a scolding,
And sitting in a corner to commit
Irregular French verbs and poetry.
Will it not keep?  And could you not for once
Say something nice, even if it were not true?

### Sir Diarmid.

Nay; what I have to say must be said now,
Unless your hand is plighted to Tremain.

### Doris.

Say on then what you have to say, Sir Diarmid.

### Sir Diarmid.

There was some compact, as I understand—
If you knew of it, it was more than I did,
Till some few days ago—between our fathers,
That we two should be wedded.  I judge them not :
They thought they had a right to guide our fates ;
They thought, at least, that it were well to keep
The lands together ; whatsoe'er they thought,
They bound us to each other, and with cords
Hard to be borne or broken.

### Doris.

　　　　　　Yes; they put
Our hearts in pawn to ease them of their straits.

### Sir Diarmid.

No, Doris, that is what they could not do,
And that's the truth you have the right to know.
No one can bind the heart; it is as free
As air, and laughs at seals and covenants.
Our hearts they could not pledge; yours now is free,
Or given to another, not to me.
I come not then—in this I will be true—
To offer mine to you, or ask for yours,
But I can give my hand, as they would have it,
Knowing it is a poor. unworthy gift,
Almost an insult, to be thrown back to me
In very scorn.

### Doris.

       And maybe you would rather
It were returned so.

### Sir Diarmid.

          That I did not say;
But if you scorned it, I might feel the less
Scorn of myself, esteeming you the more.

### Doris.

Why should I scorn you, that you give me all
You have to give?  A man can do no more.

*Sir Diarmid.*

A man can do no more; and yet I fancy
He hardly could do less.

*Doris.*

　　　　　　　　I do not know.
But, Diarmid, for your honoured father's sake,—
Or is it for the sake of lands and gear?
We'll say the former; it sounds rather better—
You sacrifice yourself.　Then why should I,
Since sacrifice comes natural to woman,
Fall short of your example?　Frankly, you
Offer a heartless hand, as frankly I
Accept it; so we both can keep our hearts
Which, as you truly say, they could not pledge,
Or raise a sixpence on them.

*Sir Diarmid.*

　　　　　　　　Do you mean
This truly, Doris?

*Doris.*

　　　　　　Surely; wherefore not?
It's just a family arrangement, with
The pious feeling that the fifth commandment
Is rightly honoured, though the Law is broken,
Which is fulfilled by love.　They do these things
In France, and find they answer admirably:

A simple piece of business, and there needs
No more about it.

*Sir Diarmid.*

Does there need no more?
Think again, Doris.

*Doris.*

Yes! we might exchange
Rings with each other, since we keep our hearts,
Sealing our hands with that our hands do wear.
Mine is a diamond; yours an opal—is it?
Fickle, they say: but that's mere superstition.
There, now; it's settled.

*Sir Diarmid.*

Can you then be happy
With such a bargain?

*Doris.*

Why, Sir Diarmid, what
Has happiness to do with it? It's business;
And business has its profits or its losses,
And if the gain is clear, what would you more?

*Sir Diarmid.*

It's sin and certain misery.

*Doris.*

                             It is
Your own suggestion, and you surely could not
Lure me to sin and misery.  Indeed,
We manufacture sins, like yards of cloth,
By these new-fangled consciences of ours,
Framed not by nature, but by novels.  Look !
Here are our lands, that lie so close together,
Fast-bound to us and to our progeny;
I am My Lady, or shall be; you, the Laird
Of all; and each has got what each would like
To have : then, as for happiness, our hearts
Are free to seek it where it may be found.
That was your own proposal, was it not?

*Sir Diarmid.*

It's like a dream.

*Doris.*

                  But not an ugly one :
I'm not a dream, and some folk think me pretty.

*Sir Diarmid.*

I know not what to say.

*Doris.*

                  Say nothing, Diarmid.
We can imagine silent love is grand,
Which, speaking, sounds most silly.  Do not try

To utter now the feeling that is in you.
Perhaps we might just kiss each other.   Yes,
It is the custom, I believe.   Now, go.
Goodbye; don't let your mother call to-day;
To-morrow I will see her.

[Exit SIR DIARMID.

                              Now I'll have
Revenge at least, whatever come of this;
I'll break that proud girl's heart within an hour.


CHORUS.

To be outwitted so !
To see your plot which was not very deep,
Nor very noble, tumbled in a heap,
    And all your hope laid low
    By one who was less noble still,
    Yet only took you at your word,
    And led you on and on, until
    She held you as a snaréd bird,
    And while you scorned your mean resource,
    And felt you had been mocked by rule,
    You wist not whether it were worse
To seem so like a knave, or else so like a fool.


    At the strangeness of it all,
    At first, a loud hoarse laugh he raised !

O

And the shaggy big-horned cattle gazed,
Wondering, over the mossy wall:
Then for a little he paused and pondered,
Keenly revolving what to do;
And off through bracken and blaeberries
　　wandered,
Nor slackened his pace till he came in view
Of the low, green, honey-suckled manse
Beside the still salt Loch that lay as in a trance.


## ACT FOURTH.—SCENE THIRD.

CHORUS.
With a heart unquiet
　　To and fro she went,
Feeding on a diet
　　Of vague presentiment
From shadows without form, that across her soul
　were sent.

So the daisied meadows
　　Close their petals white
When the brooding shadows
　　Make the day like night,
For shadows may be burdens to us, when we live
　on light.

And she went on, pleading
He is fond and true;
In a love-light reading
All that he might do—
Pleading, but the boding fear came ever back anew.

Is it not a treason
To her love, to doubt,
And in search of reason
Thus to cast about,
The which, if she had loved aright, she well might
do without?

SCENE—*The Manse Study.*  INA (*alone*).

### Ina.

Down, wicked doubts that leap on me like hounds,
And soil me with your pawing.  Well I know,
He is the truest gentleman on earth,
Tender and brave ; and now he is my own,
And honouring all women, loves but me.
And I—I love him as a woman may,
Whose love is all her life.  Why comes he not?
This day was to deliver him, he said,
From all his cares, and make me all his care,
Who would not be a care, but comfort to him—
But hush !  I hear his step upon the gravel,

Yet hurried and uncertain.  What is wrong?
Now let me gird my soul to share his burden,
Or take it all myself, if so I may.

*Enter* SIR DIARMID.

*Sir Diarmid.*

O, Ina, shall you ever look on me
So lovingly again?

*Ina.*

Ay! every day,
And all day long, I hope, if love of mine
Can aught delight you.  But what ails you now?

*Sir Diarmid.*

O, I have been a fool, and properly
Have been befooled! for I conceited me,
I was the cleverest schemer, though an ass.
Can you forgive me, Ina?

*Ina.*

I shall hardly
Take you at your own value, nor am I
So very wise that your unwisdom needs
My pardon.

*Sir Diarmid.*

But it does.  And what is more,
Until I have your pardon—and a blank one,

To be filled up by utter idiocy
Of mine—I cannot even tell you, Ina,
The thing you have forgiven.

### *Ina.*

                    Well ; I think
My heart could anything forgive to you,
Except a change in yours.

### *Sir Diarmid.*

                    And that is still
The same, has never wavered, nor yet shall,
Though I have wandered in a brain-sick dream
Of mere delusion.  One thing more, and then
You shall know all my madness.  Can you dare
To be a poor man's wife?

### *Ina.*

                    Dare to be poor !
Nay, I have feared to be a rich man's wife,
Being a poor man's daughter.  Wooden quaichs
Come handier to my use than silver goblets,
And sometimes I have trembled when I thought
My homely ways might shame you.  But what
    mean you?

*Sir Diarmid.*

No matter now; I'll tell you by and by.

*Ina.*

Nay, but if you do hint that for my sake
This lot must come to you, I could not be
A wife to make you poor.

*Sir Diarmid.*

　　　　　　　O! with your love
I shall be rich, and never shall regret.

*Ina.*

It is not your regret I fear to meet—
You are too noble—but it is my own.
The thought that I had lowered him I loved,
Or that I was a burden to his life,
Or that he might have held a higher place
And played a greater part but for my sake,
That would quite crush me.　To be poor, I heed
　　not,
But to cause poverty—I dare not do it.

*Sir Diarmid.*

Yet what if, lacking you, my life were poorer
And meaner than the meanest, having you,
Replenished with the only wealth I care for?

*Ina.*

You glorify the thing you're fain to have,
As poets glorify their favourite flowers,
Although but common daffodils.   Yet one
Can know one's self as none else can, and judge
With less imagination.   Let that pass.
But what is this you speak of?   How should you
Be poorer for your choice, but that the choice
Is a poor one enough?

*Sir Diarmid.*

              It is not that
Will make me poor.   You are my only wealth
Now, and because you are my all, I cling
The more to you.   For had I never seen
The face I deem the fairest on this earth,
Nor known the heart I prize above all treasures,
This fate had still been mine.   It must be mine,
Whether you share and sweeten it to me,
Or let me bear my burden all alone.
The thing that I must do to keep my place
I could not do, except with self-contempt,
And open-eyed dishonour, and the loss
Of all in life that makes it worth the living;
And yet I have been fooled into a promise
To do this very thing.

*Ina.*

You frighten me.
I do not understand.  What have you done?
'Tis sin to break a promise; yet it may be
A greater sin to keep it; and between
The choice of sins, 'tis hard to pick one's way.

*Sir Diarmid.*

Ay, truly it is but a choice of wrongs.
I made a promise that was false to love,
And break it that I may be true again:
Caught in the snare which I myself had laid,
I must break from it, though I break my troth,
For only being false, can I be true.
O! I am humbled and ashamed, as well
I may be.  But you do forgive me, Ina?

*Ina.*

Yes, I forgive you.  But I am perplexed,
What is it all about?

*Enter* DORIS.

*Doris.*

O, Ina dear,
Why do you keep a dragon like that Morag,
Who cannot even nicely tell a lie
To visitors, but sends them from your door,

Gruff as a bear? (*Starting.*)   Ah! You here, Diarmid,
    are you?
Well, you are favoured, Ina.   Only think;
That both of us should turn at once to you
To be the first to hear the happy news!
Of course, he has been telling you.

*Ina.*

              I know not
What you mean, Doris.

*Doris.*

       Diarmid has not told you!
Well, that was kind to let me be the bearer
Myself of my good tidings.   Can't you guess
Why I am here so happy?

*Ina.*

            Truly no;
I am not good at riddles.

*Doris.*

          But this is not
A riddle; and I wished you so to hear it
From my own lips, and not from any stranger,
Not even from Diarmid, who of course would be
Clumsy at telling it.   Yes, yes, I see
You know his ring; he put it on my finger
An hour ago, and made me O so happy!
Now will you not congratulate me?

### Sir Diarmid.

Ina,
Hear me.  Nay, do not think I wish to clear
Myself.

### Ina.

Sir Diarmid, what you wish to do
Or not to do; and whether you are right
Or wrong in doing that which you have done,
'Tis not for me to say.  Why should you bring—
You, either of you—these affairs to me,
Settled between you?  Doris, I am sure
You came not here to give me any joy,
And if you wished to pain me, you have failed,
And lost your errand.  Now, I pray you leave me;
I have much work to do in briefest time.
I hope that you will be a loving wife
And loyal; but these things concern not me.
Adieu !

### Sir Diarmid.

No, Ina, you must hear me out.
You should have heard the story from myself
Ere now, but that I shrank from my own shame,
And from your pain to hear it.  Listen then.
This lady has a right to all my land—
An honourable right by bond of law—

Unless I marry her; and I who had
No right to use such mean diplomacy,
Plotted to make her love another man,
And get refusal of my own request,
Not for her love, for that I never asked,
But for her hand, the which I did not want.
Yet she accepted that which was in truth
An offered insult—marriage without love
Frankly avowed.  I thought—nay, if you will,
I hoped that she would cast it back with scorn,
As it deserved.  O the blind fool I am!
But she picked up the gage, even so conditioned
As any woman with a woman's heart
Would have despised to touch it.  No, I do not
Accuse her to you, or defend myself.
I have done that a man will scorn himself
All his life long for doing.

*Doris.*

        Handsome terms
For one who, unsolicited, besought
My hand an hour ago!  You shall not mend
Matters in this way, sir.

*Sir Diarmid.*

        I do not hope
To mend them, but to end them.  Hear me out;

Frankly I do accept the poverty
My father has bequeathed me, and I came,
Ina, to you to tell you this resolve.


*Doris (singing).*

"The king says to the beggar maid,
    I'll clothe me too in duds,
And we'll go mending pots and pans,
    And camping in the woods."
O rare idyllic love in tattered rags!


*Sir Diarmid.*

Ina, I was a fool, and dealt in craft,
Only to be the greater fool, the more
Crafty I seemed; there is an end of that.
Doris, there is the ring you put on me,
Unasked.


*Doris.*

            We made exchange, and for myself
I'll keep what I have got.  I am not one
To throw away a lover or his lands,
While I have wits to hold them.


*Sir Diarmid.*

                    Be it so;
Take or refuse, it matters not to me:

My choice is made.  From henceforth I will be
Honest, however poor.  And—pardon me—
I had no right to insult you with an offer
Which you, perhaps in mockery, accepted,
Which I, at any rate, in simple manhood
Ought never to have made.  Take all my rights,
    then ;
They're justly yours—my house and lands and all
My fathers did enjoy; but understand
You have no right in me for evermore.


### *Ina.*

Ah ! that is right, whatever else was wrong.


### *Doris.*

O yes, of course he'll give up all for you.


### *Ina.*

'Tis nought to me.  I have no interest
In any of these doings.  Only I
Would grieve to think of one I reckoned true
And noble above many, falling from
The ideal of a better life, to be
A scorn unto himself.  But fare you well.

### *Doris.*

O, it is all the high heroics here:
The very air is tragical: we stalk
And strut, when other folk would only walk.
Moral-sublime's the *rôle!*  Cast to the wind
Houses and lands and honours all for love!
And yet I even dreamt you would have thanked
    me,
That I could be content to take his hand,
And leave his heart—to you.  Good morning, Ina;
Good morning, you, Sir Landless; we shall scarce
Meet again soon.                    [*Exit* DORIS.


### *Sir Diarmid.*

       Is this the end then, Ina?
You promised to forgive.


### *Ina.*

         I have forgiven;
Though this was not, I think, within the scope
Of possible thought then.  But can you forgive
Yourself as readily?


### *Sir Diarmid.*

       Have I fallen so low

In your esteem, that you should think this shame,
Like a boy's blush, shall vanish, and he scarcely
Know it was there?  I have done wrong, but from
That wrong I trust to shape a better life,
Which else had been as the poor gambler's luck
Fooling him to his ruin.

### Ina.

                    May it be so:
And if it be, there's no one will rejoice
More than I shall, to know that this has been
Only a passing cloud which we remember
Not as a cloud, but as a freshening shower
Redeeming the scorched land.

### Sir Diarmid.

                    Redeemed it shall be,
If shame can work repentance ; but resolve,
Knitting its brows, and girding for the battle,
May yet lose heart, seeing no gleam of hope
To brighten patience.

### Ina.

            There is hope of mending,
Of being once more what one failed to be.

*Sir Diarmid.*

But none of Love?  That is a broken cistern
That keeps no water for the broken heart,
Being once cracked ?

*Ina.*

                I pray you let me go :
Perhaps the broken cistern truly is
The only broken heart.  Farewell !

*Sir Diarmid.*

                            Farewell !
I will do right though this be hope's sad knell.

                        [*Exit* SIR DIARMID.

*Ina (alone).*

Ah me ! and I have lived through this, and may
Have many years of such a life to live !
No warning of it—the volcano smokes
Before it bursts in flame, but here the fire
Broke suddenly beneath me, and my world
Is blackened, scorched, and burning under foot,
And not a blade of all its former beauty,
And not a little well of all its gladness
Remains, and no horizon to its darkness
Except a far-off grave !  O weary life !

O Love, there is no joy like that thou bringest,
Nor any grief like that thou leav'st behind,
Being gone.  God pity me!  I was so happy;
And while my heart was singing in the light
Of its great bliss, the arrow pierced it through,
And I fell prone to—this.   What must I do?
What can I do?   No, there is nought to do,
But only try to look as if the wound
Hurt me not, and to bleed on silently,
Girding a maiden's modesty about
A broken heart, that none may find it out.
I blame him not; he has been weak, not false;
At least, it was for truth that he played false;
But O, it is too hard.   God pity me,
For my glad life is turned to misery.

[Exit.

### CHORUS.

What if your Dagon, falling down, is broken,
Dagon, to whom your daily prayer was spoken,
And the sweet incense offered to betoken
    Faith that ne'er falters?

Pick up the fragments, piece them well together,
Tenderly fit them each into the other,
Raise now the Fish-god, Lord of war and weather,
    High o'er his altars.

P

Ah ! but your heart sank, shattered as he lay there
Peace you had none then, wailing all the day there,
Yet as you look now, can you go and pray there
    As you once wended ?

Once he was glorious, your gilded Dagon,
Throned on his altar, or borne upon his waggon ;
But he was broken, and how are you to brag on
    What you've just mended ?

Here were the fractures, though they're patched up
    nicely,
And he looks once more as he did precisely ;
Yet he can no more be so paradisely
    Perfect to you now.

Varnish the joinings, veil the sunshine garish,
Dim light is fittest, when the soul would cherish
As a thing sacred that which so can perish,
    Patched up anew now.

Broken her dream is, faded all the glory,
All the cloud-castle fallen a ruin hoary.
Lost too the thread, and interest of the story
    Late so entrancing.

No more may he come to her maiden vision
Robed in the splendour of a Power Elysian ;
Only a man, he, feeble of decision,
    Foolishly chancing.

## ACT FIFTH.—SCENE FIRST.

### CHORUS.

Bears still the faithful servant on her heart
  The household joys and griefs, whate'er they be:
The well-trained hireling deftly plays her part,
But clumsy service, fairer far thou art,
    Love moving thee.


"O 'tis our bargain—so much work and wage;
  No more is in the bond," as you shall find:—
Ay! but the unwrit bonds of God engage
More than is set down in the formal page,
    Or Law can bind.


" Yes! but they are a plague, and it is wrong
  To let them be too free—it spoils them quite "—

Ay, love takes liberties, but you may long
For one true heart amid a heartless throng
    On some dark night.

No love can spoil; it perfects with its touch:
  And being free hath a familiar grace,
And like a babe even sacred things will clutch;
Yet life were dull and dismal without such
    Lights on its face.

SCENE—*Post Office.* MORAG *and* MRS. SLIT.

### *Mrs. Slit.*

Och! and it iss yourself, Mrs. Morag, that will
be a sight for sore eyes, which it wass the loch
said to the hill when it came out of a month's
mist.

### *Morag.*

Your eyes do not need salve, Mrs. Slit; they
can do without me, and without the spectacles
too, for they are as keen as a hawk's, though you
are not so much younger than myself either. But
I have been very busy, and I have had my
troubles and my tempers too.

### Mrs. Slit.

Yes, yes! We are all born to troubles and tempers, as the sparks fly upward.

### Morag.

It is just like the seal I am. I get my head above the water maybe for a minute, and turn this way and that to see about me, and then I'm down to the depths again among the crabs and the tangles—that's the troubles and tempers.

### Mrs. Slit.

But Miss Ina will not have her tempers, though.

### Morag.

Will she not? But she brings out mine whatever; and it is all the same.

### Mrs. Slit.

But an angel might do that, Morag.

### Morag.

Girls are not angels, Mrs. Slit, as you would know if you had any. Angels will know their own minds, at least, and we have four and twenty minds in the four and twenty hours.

### *Mrs. Slit.*

Yes, I know.  It iss a great change to be left all alone.

### *Morag.*

But she is not more alone now than ever she was before.  For he would be always at his books and his sermons, as close as a limpet to a rock.

### *Mrs. Slit.*

That iss true, but then he wass always there, Mrs. Morag, which it just makes the difference.  My Eachan would be a useless body sitting there by the fire for years, cramped and twisted with the rheumatics.  But he wass always there to be seen to, and to be wanting this and that; and it wass not like the same house after his arm chair would be empty.  Poor thing! it iss myself that can be sorry for her.

### *Morag.*

But it is not for you, Mrs. Slit, to be calling her a poor thing, like any fisher-lass in the clachan; and her a lady, and a minister's daughter too !

### *Mrs. Slit.*

Surely she iss to be pitied, Morag, for she iss in trouble, and which iss more, she iss an orphan, and which iss more, she will have no one to look to, but that ne'er-do-well uncle who iss here to-day, and nobody knows where to-morrow, away among heathens or tinklers.   Och ! yes, she iss to be pitied.

#### *Morag.*

No, she is not to be pitied, but to be roused up, and to be told her duty, and to be respected, Mrs. Slit. And for her uncle, he will be giving her a house and a down-sitting like a duchess, when she will go to him ; and he is not to leave Glen Chroan any more.

#### *Mrs. Slit.*

It iss yourself that will be going with her then, Morag ?

#### *Morag.*

She would as ill do without me, Mrs. Slit, as the gull without the water.

#### *Mrs. Slit.*

Yes, that iss true, you have been with her all her days.   And it iss riding in your coach you will be, and living like the princes and rulers of the earth maybe.   When will you be going, now ?

#### *Morag.*

I do not know when we will be going.   I do not know if we will ever be going, and I do not want to go near a house which is no better than a heathen's, if it be not even a papist's.

### *Mrs. Slit.*

But she will have to go somewhere soon, for we will be having the new minister, and he will need the manse, no doubt, but I hear there iss no wife to come with him, whatever.

### *Morag.*

Minister! Is it the lad you would be having two Sabbaths ago you call a minister? To think she must leave her father's house for the like of him !

### *Mrs. Slit.*

What iss wrong with him, Mrs. Morag? He iss a fery pretty man, and which iss more, he hass the beautiful Gaelic.

### *Morag.*

Maybe he has: but has he the Gospel, Mrs. Slit? We used to fault the old man because he was more dainty about his words than his doctrine. But this one, he will have no doctrine at all either about God or devil. For I heard him tell Miss Ina at her own fireside that the devil was a myth of the middle age. As if he was not as busy with young folk as he is with the like of you and me, Mrs. Slit!

*Mrs. Slit.*

Och! yes, that iss true, whatever. But what iss a myth, Mrs. Morag? You should know that have lived in a minister's house so long.

*Morag.*

Do you think that I swallow dictionaries then, because I live in a minister's house? I do not know what it is. But it will be something bad, no doubt, or it would not be spoken about him, middle age or not middle age.

*Mrs. Slit.*

Yes, it will be something bad. But he hass the good Gaelic.

*Morag.*

And the devil has the Gaelic and the English too, Mrs. Slit.

*Mrs. Slit.*

That iss true too; but he will have more English, Morag.

*Morag.*

Maybe, I do not know. He has plenty Gaelic for his purpose. But is there no letter for us to-day?

#### Mrs. Slit.

Och ! yes, there will be one for Miss Ina. I am thinking it iss from the laird himself. What will be taking him to London now, when we wass all hoping he would be come to settle among his own folk ?

#### Morag.

How should I know what would take him to London ? Maybe to bring an English wife to turn up her nose at us. But why did you not tell me of the letter before ? and me wasting my time here that never gets out of doors till the bats are after the midges !

#### Mrs. Slit.

But it wass yourself never asked till this fery minute, Mrs. Morag.

#### Morag.

And what else would I be here for at this time of day ?

#### Mrs. Slit (*examining letters*).

That iss for my lady. It iss thin, and wafered, and blue paper, and will be an account, no doubt ; they are not fery welcome at the castle, I fear. There iss no hurry about that. This iss from the

gamekeeper to the factor they would be. for drown-
ing in the loch.  It can wait; he will not be caring
for letters yet, I'm thinking.  And there iss half-a-
dozen for the long-haired poet-man that will be
courting Miss Doris.  It iss a bold man he iss, or.
maybe a blind one, whatever.

*Morag.*

Who is he, Mrs. Slit?

*Mrs. Slit.*

I do not know.  But he will be getting many
letters and printed papers, and they say he iss a
great poet in the Sassenach.  But, to be sure, that
iss not like the Gaelic.

*Morag.*

Is he often with Doris then?

*Mrs. Slit.*

Och! they are like clam-shells; there is no part-
ing them.  And he will speak sense to her maybe,
but it iss just heathenish gibberish he will be talk-
ing in my shop.

*Morag.*

That will do now.  There is Ina's letter.  I have
been too long away from her.  But I was to be
sure to ask about your Oe that had the fever.

### Mrs. Slit.

Yes, she iss a kind lady, and thinks of everyone. Allisthair iss better now, and will be at the fishing again soon.

### Morag.

And how is the fishing and the whisky?

### Mrs. Slit.

Not more than usual, Morag, but always too much of the whisky, whatever.

### Morag.

Yes! They will be like Donald Levach who was drowned in a ditch; and his last words would be— You are changing the drink, and there is too much water in it, Jenny, a great deal too much water.

[*Exit* MORAG.

### CHORUS.

Truly she did not know it,
Dreamed not of humour or mirth,
Made not an effort to show it,
Travailed no whit in its birth:
Just it came to her easy,
The quaint, odd satire and fun,
Without any purpose to please ye,
Or pleasure in its being done.

Hard and grave were her features,
Though lit up with love now and then,
For laughter was not for such creatures
As sinful women and men.
It was simply the way that she reasoned,
The natural shape of her thought,
While it looked as if cleverly seasoned
With a sharp biting wit she had got.
O ye that strive to be witty,
And hunt through your brains for a quip,
When ye have caught one, in pity
Silence it straight on your lip.


## ACT FIFTH.—SCENE SECOND.

### CHORUS.

Shall not a woman insulted have her revenge on
  the man,
Mock at him, laugh at his anguish, smite with
  what weapon she can,
Cut where the wound shall be quickest, smile as
  he writhes in the dust,
Mirthful when he comes a-begging an obolus now,
  or a crust?
Does not the feeling of injury strike out seeking
  redress?

And why should the gods plant in her a passion
    she is to repress?
They know their business, and did not fashion
    our nature to be
A soft-hearted, soft-headed, milk-and-water philan-
    thropy;
There's a hard grit in it, meant for use at the
    fitting time,
That rogues and villains may know the bitter bad
    taste of crime.—
O be gentle and meek, and kiss the hand hot
    from the blow,
And stint your soul of the pleasure, the keenest
    of all that we know!
Drive the winds over the ocean, yet say to the
    mad waves, Peace!
Why should you lift up your heads now? there,
    let your murmurings cease!
Easy to say, Forgive, and lay up your wrath on
    the shelf:
But how, if you take it so tamely, shall you re-
    spect yourself?
If you're a worm to be trod on, trod on you
    shall be again;
Never a woman insipid found chivalrous spirit in
    ·men.—

So did the wild heart brood now, passioning so
    in her wrath,
And plotted to sweep her. victim ruthlessly out
    of her path.


SCENE—*Room in Cairn-Cailleach.* TREMAIN *and* DORIS.


### Doris.

Well, sir, what think you of this gear?


### Tremain.

            Think, Doris!
I am past thinking: there's a social earthquake
Shaking my world, and toppling all things down,
While darkness reigns, and mystery, and silence.
What does it mean?  There's Diarmid, on a sudden,
Off like the swallows, with no fare-you-well,
And leaving no more trace than flight of bird
Through the impassive air; his mother packing
To follow him, and not a word to explain,
But Celtic exclamations all day long.


### Doris.

So he is gone already.

*Tremain.*

                Ay, he's gone;
But why and whither has he gone, and left
His guest to seek for other quarters, just
When one was taking to the place, and felt
Its strangeness, which at first was like a dream,
Growing familiar, with a taste of life
Fresh as the salt sea breezes?

*Doris.*

                Gone already!
I did not count on that.  And she's off too,
After him, doubtless.  Much help I have got
From your fine phrases, sir.  At every point
Baffled and mocked!  I'm weary of you all,
But I will have revenge at least.

*Tremain.*

                What's all
This rage about?  It is a pretty play,
And it becomes you rarely, as indeed
All that you do becomes you; yet I like
My Doris tender more than Doris fierce,
Although the softness is more beautiful
By reason of the wrath restrained.

*Doris.*

                Pshaw! give me
Deeds and not words: I've had enough of them!
You were to get that girl out of my way.

*Tremain.*

And out of it she is : well for herself
I daresay.

*Doris.*

But not well for you, that she
Should drive off like a princess followed by
The prayers and tears of all her subjects here—
The cripples, the rheumatics, and the idiots,
Who burden this poor land.

*Tremain.*

Why ill for me ?
She has not left a legacy of these
Impotent folk to me.

*Doris.*

That's as you will.
But he who should have humbled, broken her,
And cast her from him as a thing of naught—
Well, him I could have loved; I hate her so.

*Tremain.*

And yet you went to see her lately.

*Doris.*

Yes ;
I went because I had no man to go,
And do mine errand, and to smite her with

A word should blight her life, and break her heart,
As I had hoped it would.  But with the look
Of a grand tragedy-queen she bade me be
A dutiful wife, forsooth, to my affianced,
And wear with grace what I had won by guile.

### *Tremain.*

Affianced, Doris! am I then to take
This ring from your fair finger, and put mine
Here in its room?

### *Doris.*

      You take my ring from me!
Sir Diarmid's ring!—yes, his engagement ring!
I'd sooner part with life than part with it.

### *Tremain.*

What do you mean?

### *Doris.*

      O, I forgot.  You know not
The pretty silly farce we have been playing,
Which is to end in fateful tragedy.
Diarmid came here one day, insulting me
With offer of his hand, but not his heart—
A mere wired flower to wither on my bosom—
Hoping to be refused, and keep his lands
And sweetheart too, because he heard I loved you.

As if I could not see through such a thin
Shallow device, which he did hardly colour
With any show of likelihood :

#### *Tremain.*

Of course
You did refuse him?

#### *Doris.*

No; but at a word
Frankly accepted him on his own terms ;—
Hands without hearts, vows that were lies avowed.
Would you have had me do the very thing
He hoped that I would do, and strip myself
Of all my rights that he might wed that girl?

#### *Tremain.*

Well; you accepted only as a *ruse*—
My clever Doris—meaning by and by
To wreck his hope more wholly.

#### *Doris.*

Not at all.
You poets, O how little do you know
The women, after all, you're fain to paint!
You see their eyes and hair, and hear their words:
But for their minds they are too fine for you.

Men's brains, I think, can have no convolutions,
They go at things so straight and stupid, like
A gaze-hound at a doubling hare.

### *Tremain.*

Nay, Doris,
You could not surely throw away my love.

### *Doris.*

Why should I throw away your love, because
I take an offer offering no love?
Should I not need, and prize it all the more,
That it would give me what my fate denied?
I've heard you say that love is poetry,
And marriage languid prose, that never stirs
The pulse of high imagination, having
No passionate music in it.  I must have
Some poetry in my life, and you could give it.

### *Tremain.*

Yes! So! Like verses in a magazine,
I might come in to fill a space, a blank,
Between the story and the criticism;
Not even like the Chorus in the Greek
Drama, to fill the passion up, and cry
To the stern fates for pity.  Thank you, Doris,
But love like mine will hardly serve for padding.

*Doris.*

What ails you now?  A badly written book
May have its very essence and its life
In the appendix.  And my life without you
Were dull enough with him.

*Tremain.*

                You did not mean, then,
To marry him really.

*Doris.*

                Indeed I did, and would
I should have made his life a misery
Perhaps, and seen him bitterly repent
His dirty bargain ; but we both agreed
To join our hands, and keep our hearts apart.
And really I did mean it.

*Tremain.*

                Beautiful tigress !

*Doris.*

Tigress, if you will ; but who has lost
Her spring, and turns more savage on her prey.
Look here.  I will not hide a thing from you :
We sealed our bargain by exchange of rings,
And other pretty customary forms
Of kindness and affiance ; and straightway

He hurried to that girl who set him on
To break his plighted troth : contented she
To take him in the shame of such dishonour.


*Tremain.*

How  know  you  that ?


*Doris.*

                    How  do  I  know  it ?   Why,
I found them closeted together, heard
His own false lips renounce the vow he made
An hour before.   O, he was most polite—
My gentleman !  and  did  his  villain-work
Like preaching ; for of course he had been schooled,
How best to lay the moral varnish on,
And spout fine sentiment.   I hate sentiment ;
It is the flimsiest lie that walks the earth,
The mere thin ghost of truth.   He must admit
With shame, forsooth, his offer was an insult,
And as an insult humbly he withdrew it :
He would not mock a lady with the boon,
If boon it could be called, of loveless marriage :
But frankly he had hoped I would reject it,
Which now he was ashamed of like the rest.
The moral prig !  as if I did not know
Where  he  had  learnt  his  lesson !

*Tremain.*

> So he parted
With house and lands and honours all for love.

*Doris.*

And you too! You take up the tragic style
To glorify a fool!

*Tremain.*

> Yes, for I could
Give all the world, too, just to win your love.

*Doris.*

Not long ago you said I was a tigress.

*Tremain.*

Even so; a grand and proud and terrible beauty,
A matchless strength of passion good or evil,
Like a volcano, having on its slopes
Fair vineyards here, there burning lava-floods.
And howsoe'er you show, you do transfix
My soul with admiration.

*Doris.*

> Oh! Perhaps
You think my fires have burnt up Diarmid's share
And now the sunny slopes are for your vines.

*Tremain.*

Why not? You know that poets always were
Alike the favourites of the gods and demons;
And he is gone whom you did never love,
While I am here whom you have said you loved.
What then will you do next?

*Doris.*

          I will pull down
Each stone of that old house, and scatter all
The gatherings of ages—pictures, tapestries,
Arms, chinas, books, and nick-nacks, every heirloom
And symbol of their greatness, sending them
Where never can he hope by any chance
To pick them up again: and then I'll make
A forest of the place, and stalk the deer
Over his threshold.

*Tremain.*

          You are thorough, Doris.

*Doris.*

Ay! he shall find that, who has flouted me.

*Tremain.*

Where is he now?

*Doris.*

          Nay, you should know that best.

### Tremain.

I know not.  There is only Celtic wailing
All through the house, and I have found a shelter
Down in the village.

### Doris.

                        He is gone at least ;
And she, too, is away—perhaps with him.

### Tremain.

Nay, she went with her uncle yester eve ;
I saw her go, and thought her looking pale.

### Doris.

O yes ! you take a mighty interest,
Like others, in her movements and her looks !
Perhaps, too, you are fain to sacrifice—
If you have any such to offer up—
Houses and lands and honour for her love.
By all means do: you have my full consent
To play the fool as he did.

### Tremain.

                        I could play
The fool indeed like him, but not for her :
I think I am even more a fool than he,
Clinging as for dear life to one who bids me

Go seek another love.  You know well, Doris,
'Tis easy saying to the captive, Go,
When he is bound and fettered.

*Doris.*

My poor boy,
Are you so deep enthralled ?  But what was that
You said about an uncle?  She has none.
Her father had a brother once in India
Was something to my father—Agent, Factor—
What not ?—a scant-o'-grace and ne'er-do-well.
But he is dead, O, years and years ago.

*Tremain.*

I tell but what I heard.  Some one at least
Carried her off last night.  I saw them go ;
They said he was her uncle.  Enough of her.
I know not why you should so hate her, Doris,
Or so hate anything.  'Tis so much better
To love, which sweetens all things like a flower.

*Doris.*

Ay ! better truly for your sluggish souls,
Which, like your English rivers, creep along
Oily and dull and muddy.  But for me
My love is hotter than can boil in your
Slow veins, and yet I hate more heartily
Than I can love.

*Tremain.*

When shall I call you mine,
Doris?  Then you shall see how I can love.

*Doris.*

Why, that you call me twenty times a day.

*Tremain.*

Nay, do not trifle.  Let us fix the time,
Since there is nought to come between us now.

*Doris.*

O, fixing times is stupid.  I should hate
The day I fixed, and change it in a week.
Or, when it came, should keep my bed, and sleep
Its hours away, unnoted.  But I thought
You were content to love, and held that marriage
Was like the lump of ice in the champagne,
Cooling and weakening passion.

*Tremain.*

Then I knew not
The agony and ecstasy of love,
The rapture and the misery of hope,
The jealous watching through the troubled nights,
And sinking of the heart.  Say when.

*Doris.*

         I cannot.
Maybe a year hence I may settle in
The dull jog-trot of marriage—maybe never.
Who knows what is to happen?  I'm content
Meanwhile that things should go on as they do.

*Tremain.*

You cannot love like me, then.

*Doris.*

         Go away!
I cannot babble sentiment, and coin
My heart into a ballad to be sold
To publishers, and sung by silly maids.
And if you are not satisfied with that
Which I can give you, there are lots of girls
Will lend their ears to hear your dainty speeches,
And even to believe them—they're such fools.

           [*Exit.*

CHORUS.

So she let him go,
 Puffing him away,
Like a flimsy bubble,
Never more to trouble
 Her upon her way.

So she let him go,
  Back to his old gods,
Jove and Aphrodite,
Thor and Odin mighty,
  And his songs and odes.

So she let him go
  To fulfil his bent
In his pagan ethic
And his fond æsthetic,
  And his self-content.

So she let him go
  With a mocking smile;
Yet no heart was broken
When her words were spoken,
  Though he moped a while.


## ACT FIFTH.—SCENE THIRD.

### Chorus.

Ai me! ai me!
Fate sits upon the steed
Behind the soul whose passion holds the reins;
Ai me! ai me!
Better the bending reed,

When the gods thunder, than the oaks and planes.
The  reed  remains,  when  their  proud  strength  is
    shattered.


Ai me ! ai me !
There's madness in the cup
Which jealous wrath mingles in hellish spite ;
Ai me ! ai me !
And when we hold it up
It laughs and lightens gaily to the sight,
Yet in its might the might of man shall perish.


SCENE—*Room in Cairn-Cailleach.*  DORIS, DR. LORNE,
*and* BENNETT.


### *Doris.*

What would you, gentlemen ?  My time is brief.
You ask an interview, and fix the time,
Nor wait to know my poor convenience.
No matter.  Only let us to the point
Without preliminary phrasing.  My
Mare yonder waits for me, and grows impatient.


### *Bennett.*

We have a little business——

*Doris.*

                              Business ! O !
Here is my factor coming, and he does
All business for me.

                    *Enter* FACTOR.

                              Let me introduce you.


*Bennett.*

Happy to know the gentleman; but we
Crave audience of yourself for this affair,
Which he can scarcely order, not at least
Till you shall give him your authority
Express.  Yet it is well he should be here
To counsel you.


            *Dr. Lorne.*

            Miss Cattanach, of course
You got the papers which I forwarded,
And so far are prepared for us.


                    *Doris.*

                              And pray
Who is this peremptory gentleman ?


            *Dr. Lorne.*
My name is Lorne—a friend once of your father's.

*Doris.*

I've heard of such a person—but he died;
Was drowned, or drowned himself—I forget which;
But people said it would be a relief
To all his kinsfolk.  Any friend of his?

*Dr. Lorne.*

Only himself, come back to plague his friends
Who hoped he had relieved them of his presence,
And who will welcome him like other ghosts
That can't lie quiet in their graves.  And now
About those papers, Miss?

*Doris.*

　　　　　　　What papers?　O!
That trumped-up story of his being alive,
And claiming monies trusted to my father
Years ago.  Yes, I think the papers came.
I did not read them; they are too absurd,
And you may have them back now if you like.
They're somewhere i' the waste-basket.  I'm advised
To prosecute you for conspiracy,
If you are he that sent them; but the writer
Is fitter sure for bedlam.

*Dr. Lorne.*

　　　　　　　You are well
Acquainted with their purport, for a person

Who never read them.  As I never doubt
A lady's word, I must conclude you knew
The facts already.  That will shorten matters.

### Bennett.

Listen, Miss Cattanach; these are grave affairs;
And with a kindly purpose we are here
To choke a painful scandal in the birth,
If so we may.  You could not overlook
Those documents.

### Doris.

   Well, no; I told a lie,
A stupid one too.  Yes, I read the trash
With laughter as it merited.  It seems
You'd rob my father of his honest name—
Who, you say, was your friend—when he is dead,
And cannot answer for himself; and next
You would rob me, and being but a woman
Weak-nerved of course, you point your pistol at me,
Shotted with stuff incredible, demanding
My money or my life—brave highway-man!
Pray you now, pull the trigger, sir, and see
If I shall wince.

### Dr. Lorne.

  So that's your line.  And now
Your factor here, does he approve of it?

R

### Doris.

Sir, I can manage my affairs as yet;
I am of age, and not quite fatuous;
But you can ask him.

### Factor.

Yes, I do endorse

All that my lady says.

### Dr. Lorne.

So be it, then;

There's no more to be said, I apprehend.
Come, Bennett, let us go.

### Bennett.

Nay, not so fast.

Do not by haste or wrangling further snarl
A knot already hard to disentangle.
My fair young lady, you can hardly know
The chances or the certainties of Law;
But if I had a little while alone
Now with your agent, I could make it plain
He gives you ill advice.

### Doris.

No doubt, you two

Being closeted together for an hour

Would order all my life.   But I prefer
To shape it for myself.

### Factor.

                    And I would leave
The Law to give to every one his due.

### Doris.

As your friend says, I think there needs no more.
This gentleman who went and drowned himself
To benefit his family, that did not
Profit much by his living, turns up now
Modestly asking eighty thousand pounds,
With interest and compound interest
For ten or twelve years past.   But since the payment
Of all these monies would go far indeed
To beggar me, he is content if I
Will give up to Sir Diarmid house and lands
Now forfeited to me.

### Dr. Lorne.

                    Ay, so I wrote
In that same paper which you did not read,
And have so clearly understood.

### Doris.

                    O yes !
I understand it better than you think :

As thus: I read between the lines that you
Have made a covenant to wed your niece,
Miss Lorne, with Diarmid, who is my betrothed,
But by her counsel falsely breaks his word.
Now hear me.  I will fight it to the last,
And will not stint my vengeance, though I starve
My life to feed it.  I believe your stories
Are lies from first to last about my father,
From first to last inventions to entrap
Poor Diarmid in your snares.  But were they all
As true as they are false, as credible
As they are clean impossible, it would not
Matter to me.  That girl shall never sit
My lady in his house, and smile and fawn
Upon the man whose plighted troth I wear,
See, on my finger.  There; you have my answer.
Our business now is ended.                    [*Exit.*

*Dr. Lorne.*

           A high-stepping
Filly, that now.  But though her tongue is sharp,
And she has touched me somewhat on the raw,
I bear no grudge, if she had only left
Ina alone.  I like a clever girl
With pluck and talent.

*Bennett.*

  Was there ever creature
So reckless and unreasonable as
An angry woman?

*Dr. Lorne.*

  Well, I do not know.
She means to get from life the thing she wants,
Cost what it may, as your philosopher
Will burn his diamond just to prove 'tis nought
But charcoal, and we call him wise.  It all
Comes to the same at last.  One toils for fame,
And from his garret where he gnaws a crust
Scorns your respectable folk; another swings—
I've seen them—on a hook whose iron digs
Into the flesh, and he too laughs at us
Who live by reason; she is fain to have
Revenge for love insulted; and perhaps
Each gets as much from life i' the end as we
Who gather wealth, and think that they are mad.
Only the pursuit pleases; the possession
Is empty or bitter always.  But these aims
Have most intense delight, and in their failure
A kind of tragic grandeur.  That girl now
Has lived, within this hour, as much at least
As three good years of our lives.

*Bennett.*

Fiddlesticks !
She is a fool, sir, and her sentiments
Are heathenish or even devilish.

[*Looks out of window.*

Look at her ;
She'll drive that horse mad if she curb him so,
And lash him in her tantrums.

*Dr. Lorne.*

Ah ! that's bad.
Now, if she were a friend of mine, she should not
Ride off alone, for horse and rider have
A wild eye in their heads.  She cannot mean
To take the old hill-road on such a brute.
Yes ! there she gallops up the rocky path,
Past the old mill, at every hoof a brush
Of fiery sparks ; she's near the ash-tree now
That sends a low branch right across the way.
By Jove ! she's taken it like a fence, and crashed
Right through the twigs and leaves.  Well ridden,
    girl !
Now, could I but throw off some forty years,
I'd risk a ride through life with such a mate.
She's out of sight now.  There's an ugly bit
Of road along the crags, above Loch Dhu.
What's that ?  I could be sworn it was a scream ;

And there's no tramp of hoofs now: it is fallen
Terribly silent.

*Bennett.*
> Let us go and see.


CHORUS.

Up the steep path on the hill,
Past the wild race of the mill,
Leaping o'er branch and boulder-stone
Madly the rider galloped on.
And up to the heights of that rocky road,
Mad as her rider, the sorrel strode,
While her sharp ears were forward turned,
And the quick smoke from her nostrils burned,
And the evil white from her eye had fled,
But it was blood-shot now instead,
As she swept past a twisted, grey,
Ghostly root where a young lamb lay,
Picked till each several rib was bare
By hungry ravens that haunted there.

There were two lovers whispering low
  Among the bracken beside the brook,
Where the juniper bush, and the ragged sloe
  Made for lovers a sheltered nook:

There were two ravens that did croak
    Over the lamb's ribs picked so bare;
Was there no weakling of the flock
    To make them another supper there?
Clatter, clatter upon the rock,
    They heard the hoofs of the Sorrel ring,
Only a muffled thud they woke
    Now and then on the moss or ling.
Lovers and ravens then upsprung,
    As nearer and nearer it came with speed,
And a wild shriek 'mong the echoes rung,
    But it was not the woman, it was the steed.
What had happened?  All now was still,
    Only the raven, hopping slow
To a giddy ledge of the rocky hill,
    Kept peering down on the depths below.


## ACT FIFTH.—SCENE FOURTH.

### CHORUS.

A low-arched bridge,
All tufted green with moss and maiden-hair,
        Spanned a slow stream
        That lapsed as in a dream

Through sedge and willow and meadow flat and fair;
And all around were great hills, shadowy, sharp,
  and bare.


On many a knoll,
Silent the golden plovers kept their seat,
  And in the stream
  That lapsed as in a dream
The heron slumbered, cooling breast and feet,
And you could see the air all tremulous with heat.


Ah ! our unrest
More restless grows when all around is peace;
  For life doth seem
  To lapse as in a dream
Which hath not any fruit or due increase,
And we do fret the more that the calm doth not
  cease.


O low-arched bridge
With tinted moss and dainty fern o'ergrown,
  And thou slow stream,
  Lapsing as in a dream,
More hateful ye than perilous stepping stone
And turbid river, since peace from her heart has
  flown.

Scene—*Bridge near Glen Chroan Lodge.*   Ina *and* Morag.

*Ina.*

This is the land of sleep; here no man works
Or thinks.

*Morag.*

   The women work.

*Ina.*

    O yes, they toil
'Neath heavy burdens, while their lords, forsooth,
Lie in the sun and watch them sweltering.
I could not live here, Morag; it is like
A life in death, oblivious listlessness
That nothing cares for, and remembers nought.
See, the slow brook creeps sleepily along,
The trout are slumbering yonder in the pools.
The cows lie on the grass with closed eyelids,
Languidly chewing, and the yellow bees
Wheel drowsily about.  These inland lakes
Are not like our sea-lochs; there's life in them,
Motion and waves and pulsing of the tide,
And on their shores we know that we are near
The world's great highway thronged with busy life.

*Morag.*

You used to call Loch Thorar sleepy too.

*Ina.*

Ay, so it is, compared with busy streets
Where eager industries do push and drive,
And hurrying throngs answer the ringing bells,
And huge unwearying machineries
Are waited on by patient servitors,
Like gods that must be tended morn and eve.
There men and women work, and life is lived
At the full pitch, for there each man is kept
Strict to his task at book or saw or yardstick,
Or whatsoe'er his tool be, by the vast
Machine of civilization.

*Morag.*

                I am thinking
That no one wants to be just where he is;
We're fain to kick our shadows from our feet,
As we might do our slippers.

*Ina.*

                Maybe so;
And yet I willingly would lose myself
In work which is not wholly for myself,
And thought which is not all about myself.
Yes, I am weary of that.

*Morag.*

              But there's your uncle:
Might you not work, and think a bit for him?

### Ina.

He will not let me.  He is all for wrapping
A girl in cotton-wadding to be kept
Like a wax-doll.  He is my slave to fetch
And carry for me: I am his morning thought,
His daily task too, and his evening care.
I must not let the sun freckle my skin,
Nor yet the night lamp weary my poor eyes,
Toiling at book or needlework or music.
'Tis always *Me* that must be thought about,
And I am sick of Me.  Where did he learn
His notions about women?  In the East
Among Zenanas?  They are worse, I think,
Than our rough crofters' ways.

### Morag.

      He's very good;
You should be grateful, Ina.

### Ina.

      Grateful, yes!
But then to live is more than to be nursed
And tended like a baby.  What am I,
To get all this observance and respect?
I want to be at work.  This idleness
Is like the waste of water-power among

Our hills, which might have brought the people
    bread.


*Morag.*

You're weary of being an idol to be worshipped;
And they do say a woman's soul was meant
Rather to worship man, and maybe guide him
To make him worshipful.  Are you sure, Ina,
It is the worship or the guiding of him
That you have dreamt of?


*Ina.*

           O, all that is past.
There was a time of fond idolatry
When I did shrine an image in my heart,
And never wearied burning incense to it,
And offering sacrifice, and singing lauds,
And building temples of imagination
For other votaries.  That time is gone.
The glory and the beauty and the dream
Are vanished; and the fire is burnt to ashes
That choke when they are stirred.  I have no wish
Either to guide or worship, since the stream
That sang along my path amid the flowers
Is all gone dry and muddy and common-place.
God help me !

*Morag.*

　　　　　Ina, one day I was sailing
By misty Morven in the early morning,
And as I looked I saw upon the mist
My shadow, and the shadows of all the rest,
And they were only shadows flitting dim,
But on my head there seemed a golden crown
Flashing with diamonds.  So it was with all;
Each saw a halo circling his own head,
And all his neighbours only common shadows;
So is the vanity of youthful dreams.

*Ina.*

Nay, Morag, but the halo and the crown,
In my case, did not rest upon my brow,
Where vanity would put it, but on his;
And now there is no glory anywhere,
But work might bring forgetfulness.

*Morag.*

　　　　　　　But, Ina,
Where can you go that trouble will not come?
You stand upon the beach, and there the waves
Tumble and foam, and, looking seaward, you
Are sure that all is bright and calm and sunny,
Till you are there.

### Ina.

But there, at least, you find
Ropes to be hauled, and sails to reef, and waves
To battle with; and I would, like the sailor,
Rather a gale of wind than lie becalmed.
But there; enough of me and my affairs.
Have you heard aught of Kenneth lately?

### Morag.

Ay!

Kenneth, poor lad, will never sing again;
His pipe is like the blackbird's hoarse and rusty,
Just as the summer comes.

### Ina.

How do you mean?

### Morag.

You know that he and Mairi were together
Sitting among the bracken on the height
When Doris took her last mad ride along
The old hill road. 'Twas they that brought the tidings
How her horse shied there at a sudden turn
Upon the ridge, seeing a raven leap
From a dead lamb that he had picked all bare.
They said the boy looked scared.

*Ina.*

                    I do not wonder.
It was a scene of horror.

                    *Morag.*
                              Yes ; but now
He says that, hearing that wild tramp of hoofs
Along the rocky path where never horse
Was known to gallop yet, he started up
Just as she reached the perilous turn o' the road ;
And he will have it that his sudden rising,
And not the raven, scared the frantic brute,
Whose labouring flanks were white with creamy
     foam,
And its eyes red with blood, so that it made
The fatal step, and stumbled o'er the brink
Of dark Craig-dhu.

                    *Ina.*
                    It might be so, and yet
No blame to him.

                    *Morag.*
                    But he will blame himself.
And then his Mairi is the heir of all
Her cousin's wealth, and she, he says, could never
Wed him that murdered Doris, nor can he
Touch gold that is so stained with blood.

*Ina.*

>                         Poor lad !

And what does Mairi say?

*Morag.*

>                         She sits by him,

E'en like a patient dove beside its mate
That lies a-bleeding, croodling softly to him,
And glad to put her heritage away,
If he will smile again; and that he cannot.

*Ina.*

Ah me! what threads of sorrow everywhere
Run through this tangled life!   But go now, Morag.
Here comes my uncle.

>             [*Exit* MORAG *and enter* DR. LORNE.

*Dr. Lorne.*

>                         Ina, it is done,

The job you wished, and as you wished it done;
Yet a bad job, I fear.

*Ina.*

>                         Nay, I am sure

'Tis the right thing, and the right way to do it.
No other way was possible.   Does he know?

### Dr. Lorne.

He knows that, when a search was duly made,
No deed was found such as he had supposed,
And so there is no burden on his land,
Or claimant for it.  It has touched his heart
With some remorseful thoughts about that girl.

### Ina.

That's as it should be.  It is best for us,
And keeps our hearts the sweeter, that the lights,
Lingering about the grave, are soft and tender.
But he suspects no more—nothing behind.

### Dr. Lorne.

Nothing.  I wish he did.  It is not right
This virtue unrewarded, lavishing
Wealth on a man who writes in melting mood
Of her that wronged him, with no recognition
Of her who set all right.  It is too fine
For my taste.  'Tis as God had done his work,
And let the devil take all the credit of it,
Which God himself objects to.

### Ina.

　　　　　　Yet it could not
Be otherwise, for he's a gentleman,
And could not take a gift like this from me.

There was no way except to burn her claim
And yours in the same fire, so blotting out
That chapter, as it never had been writ.

### Dr. Lorne.

I don't know that.  He could have taken you,
And the rest with you.  Men are not so nice
And dainty about marrying money, when
It is a handsome girl that's freighted with it.
There was no need to tell him his good fortune
Till the day after.

### Ina.

That is past for ever.

### Dr. Lorne.

For ever's not a word for woman's lips,
Nor a man's either.  I have sworn it oft,
And every time I swore I had to break
My oath.  For Ever—Never, that belongs
To God alone, who does not change His mind.

### Ina.

Does he return here soon?

### Dr. Lorne.

Yes, I suppose so.
He says that he has found that he can work,
But that he has not found his proper work:

That's here among his people—not in London.
I don't know what he means.  There's nothing here
For man to do but shoot and fish and grumble.

*Ina.*

O, he will find his task in life, and now,
Uncle, you'll take me hence.  For me at least,
There is no work here.

*Dr. Lorne.*
Whither would you, Ina?

*Ina.*

Anywhere, anywhere ; but away from this.

*Dr. Lorne.*
What say you, then, to Italy?

*Ina.*
Italy !
I never thought of that.  Yes ! let us go,
And see the picture-galleries and statues,
The Temples of the gods, the Colosseum,
The towns perched on the hills among the olives,
The castles, and the ancient civic grandeur
Of merchants who were princes ruling states—
All that you oft have told me about Rome

And Venice and Verona and fair Florence.
I am so useless, and I wish to learn,
And Italy's a book with many a page
Wondrously written, and illuminate
With golden letters.  Yes, we will go there.

### CHORUS.

At fair Ravenna, one day, she was taking
  Rest near the wharves where once rose many a
    mast,
But now the goats their pasture there are making,
And the grey sea-waves miles away are breaking,
  As her life too had ebbed far from its past.

Sadly she gazed on palace, cot, and tower,
  And mused upon the Empire's fading days,
And on Theodoric and the Lombard power,
The rush of barbarous peoples, and the dower
  Of beauty that transformed their rude old ways.

But ever with the thought of these old ages
  Thoughts of a nearer past would mingle still,
Thoughts of her fruitless work and empty wages,
And yesterday would write upon the pages
  Of History, and all their margin fill.

And as the yellow bee was drowsy humming,
  And drowsily the convent bells would ring,
And at a neighbouring lattice one was strumming
A poor guitar, she knew that he was coming,
  And a new future surely opening.

Nought had she heard of him or of his doing,
  Yet she was sure that he was near at hand,
That he came swift as one who goes a-wooing,
And trembling as an eager soul pursuing
  The quest of something he deemed pure and
    grand.

"Ina," he whispered, at her feet low kneeling,
  Nor did she startle, only answered low:
"I knew that you had come. I had the feeling;
And past is past." And then their lips were sealing,
  Forever now, the love of long ago.

THE END.

GLASGOW: ROBERT MACLEHOSE,
Printer to the University·

# 𝔓𝔬𝔢𝔪𝔰 𝔟𝔶 𝔱𝔥𝔢 𝔰𝔞𝔪𝔢 𝔄𝔲𝔱𝔥𝔬𝔯.

OLRIG GRANGE : a Poem in Six Books.   Third Edition.   Ex. fcap. 8vo.   6s. 6d.

" This remarkable poem will at once give its anonymous author a high place among contemporary English poets.—*Examiner.*

" The most sickening phase of our civilization has scarcely been exposed with a surer and quieter point, even by Thackeray himself, than in this advice of a fashionable and religious mother to her daughter."—*Pall Mall.*

" The story is told in powerful and suggestive verse."—*Spectator.*

" The pious self-pity of the worldly mother, and the despair of the worldly daughter are really brilliantly put.   The story is worked out with quite uncommon power."—*Academy.*

" The author of ' Olrig Grange' stepped at once, on the publication of that remarkable book, to a high place among the poets of the time."—*Scotsman.*

---

NORTH COUNTRY FOLK.   Poems by Author of "Olrig Grange."   Ex. fcap. 8vo.   7s. 6d.

" These poems are really dramatic, genuinely pathetic, and will bear reading over and over again."—*Westminster Review.*

" The follies and pettiness of suburban life provoke Dr. Smith's scorn. The race for wealth, the desire for position, and other kindred themes, are treated in a straightforward, outspoken fashion."—*Dundee Advertiser.*

" ' Wee Curly Pow' is full of exquisite pathos and tenderness, and 'Dick Dalgleish' is rich in genuine humour.   We recommend all who are fond of genuine poetry to get Dr. Smith's poems at once.   The book is full of music."—*Sheffield Independent.*

" For rich variety alike in substance and form, for scathing exposure of all that is mean and base, and for the effective presentation of the loftiest ideals, for mingled humour and pathos, we do not know a volume in the whole range of Scottish verse that can be said to surpass ' North Country Folk'."—*Christian Leader.*

HILDA ; AMONG THE BROKEN GODS : a Poem.   By the Author of "Olrig Grange." Third Edition.   Extra fcap. 8vo.  7s. 6d.

"That it is characterized by vigorous thinking, delicate fancy, and happy terms of expression, is admitted on all hands."—*Times.*

"A poem of remarkable power.   It contains much fine thought, and shows throughout the deepest penetration into present-day tendencies in belief or no-belief."—*British Quarterly Review.*

"It is to 'Hilda,' however, that we must turn for the most tragic conception of actual life that has hitherto been fashioned into verse.  No modern poet, it may safely be said, has plunged so deeply into the innermost heart of living men and women, and none has used such remarkable materials for his drama."—*Scottish Review.*

"This is a noble poem, very tragic and full of beauties.  The rhythm throughout is exquisite, and the colouring delicious.  The humour is peculiar—the sarcasm grim and cutting."—*Metropolitan.*

"This remarkable poem.  .  .  .  To use the words of Milton, the tale of 'Hilda' is told in language which is at once simple, sensuous, and passionate.  We have not read for some considerable time a poem which is more rivetting in interest."—*Spectator.*

"The author understands how to tell a story in rhyme and tell it in musical verse.  He knows how to portray the humours and follies of the hour."—*Pall Mall Gazette.*

"'Hilda' could only have been produced by a writer of great intellectual gifts."—*Scotsman.*

BORLAND HALL : a Poem.   By the Author of "Olrig Grange."
[*Third Edition in preparation.*

RABAN ; OR, LIFE SPLINTERS : a Poem.   By the Author of "Olrig Grange."          [*Second Edition in preparation.*

## JAMES MACLEHOSE & SONS, GLASGOW.

# Catalogue of Books

PUBLISHED BY

# JAMES MACLEHOSE & SONS,

Publishers to the University of Glasgow.

GLASGOW: 61 ST. VINCENT STREET.

1884.

PUBLISHED BY

## JAMES MACLEHOSE AND SONS, GLASGOW,

**Publishers to the University.**

---

### MACMILLAN AND CO., LONDON AND NEW YORK.

London, . . . . Hamilton, Adams and Co.
Cambridge, . . . Macmillan and Bowes.
Edinburgh, . . . Douglas and Foulis.

---

AUGUST, MDCCCLXXXIV.

PUBLISHERS TO THE
UNIVERSITY OF GLASGOW.

# Messrs. MACLEHOSE'S
# Catalogue of Books.

ALEXANDER, Patrick, M.A.—CARLYLE REDIVIVUS. Being an Occasional Discourse on Sauerteig. Fourth Edition. Crown 8vo. 1s.

"Exceedingly witty."—*Saturday Review.*
"A cleverer parody has not appeared since the 'Rejected Addresses.'"—*Manchester Courier.*

ANDERSON—ON THE CURABILITY OF ATTACKS OF TUBERCULAR PERITONITIS AND ACUTE PHTHISIS. By T. M'CALL ANDERSON, M.D., Professor of Clinical Medicine in the University of Glasgow. Crown 8vo. 2s. 6d.

ANDERSON—LECTURES ON MEDICAL NURSING, delivered in the Royal Infirmary, Glasgow. By J. WALLACE ANDERSON, M.D., Lecturer on Medicine. Second Edition. Fcap. 8vo. 3s. 6d.

"An admirable guide. . . . In many respects the best manual we at present possess on the subject. The book is carefully written. The style is clear and attractive, and the arrangement of the matter is admirable."—*Lancet.*
"The very important subjects these lectures discuss are severally treated with clearness, precision and sound judgment."—*Spectator.*
"Dr. Anderson's admirable little book contains just such information as every nurse should possess, and this is seasoned with much wise advice and many good maxims."—*Birmingham Medical Review.*
"A valuable text book. Throughout his instructions Dr. Anderson is always practical and clear."—*Health.*

ANDREWS—THE PSYCHOLOGY OF SCEPTICISM AND PHENO-MENALISM. By JAMES ANDREWS. Crown 8vo. 2s. 6d.

ARGYLL, Duke of—WHAT THE TURKS ARE. 8vo. 1s.

BANNATYNE—GUIDE TO THE EXAMINATIONS FOR PRO-MOTION IN THE INFANTRY. Containing Questions and Answers on Regimental Duties. PART I. Ranks of Lieutenant and Captain. By LIEUTENANT-COLONEL BANNATYNE. Eighteenth Edition. Crown 8vo. 7s.

BANNATYNE—GUIDE FOR PROMOTION. PART II. Rank of Major. Fourteenth Edition. Crown 8vo. 7s.

BANNATYNE—INSTRUCTIONS FOR THE PAYMENT OF TROOPS AND COMPANIES IN THE CAVALRY AND INFAN-TRY. Small 8vo. 6s.

BANNATYNE—BRIGADE DRILL. Small 8vo. 1s.

BARR—MANUAL OF DISEASES OF THE EAR, for the Use of Practitioners and Students of Medicine. By THOMAS BARR, M.D., Lecturer on Aural Surgery, Anderson's Col-lege, Glasgow. Crown 8vo, Illustrated. 10s. 6d. [*This Day.*

BATHGATE—PROGRESSIVE RELIGION. Sermons by the late REV. WILLIAM BATHGATE, D.D., Kilmarnock. Crown 8vo. 6s.

" It is impossible to read these pages without being struck by the earnestly devout spirit which characterized the preacher—a spirit which was not, however, inconsistent with a fearless pursuit of truth, wherever it was to be found."—*Leeds Mercury.*

" Those who desire to make the acquaintance of one of the master-spirits of our generation will not fail to procure this volume."—*Christian Leader.*

" The sermons convey to us the impression that we are in the presence of a Scottish Isaac Taylor—one, moreover, in whom is combined the thought-fulness of that English Christian philosopher, with a richness of the emotional nature, and an almost womanly tenderness of heart, which speaks of birth and breeding in that Border region of Scotland which is vocal with song and ballad."—*North British Daily Mail.*

BATHGATE—COLONIAL EXPERIENCES IN NEW ZEALAND. By A. BATHGATE, Dunedin. Crown 8vo. 7s. 6d.

"Pleasant, chatty, and unpretending."—*Leeds Mercury.*

BELL—AMONG THE ROCKS AROUND GLASGOW. With a Coloured Geological Map. By DUGALD BELL. Crown 8vo. 6s.

"Always careful and exact, but never dull. We have seldom seen scientific facts more happily popularized."—*North British Daily Mail.*
"May serve as an agreeable guide to any geological stranger who, finding himself in the district, cares to use his hammer 'among the rocks around Glasgow.' "—*The Academy.*

BLACK—THE LAW AGENTS' ACT 1873 : ITS OPERATIONS AND RESULTS AS AFFECTING LEGAL EDUCATION IN SCOTLAND. By WILLIAM GEORGE BLACK, Writer, Vice-President of the Glasgow Juridical Society. Crown 8vo. 2s. 6d.

"'This is a very readable booklet. We have much pleasure in commending it as a valuable addition to the literature regarding legal education in Scotland."—*Journal of Jurisprudence.*

BLACKBURN—CAW, CAW ; or, the Chronicle of the Crows : a Tale of the Spring Time. Illustrated by J. B. (MRS. HUGH BLACKBURN). 4to. 2s. 6d.

BLACKBURN—THE PIPITS. By the Author of "Caw, Caw," with Sixteen page Illustrations by J. B. 4to. 3s.

"'This is a charming fable in verse, illustrated by the well-known J. B., whose power in delineating animals, especially birds, is scarcely inferior to Landseer or Rosa Bonheur."—*Courant.*

BONAR—PARSON MALTHUS. By JAMES BONAR, B.A. Oxon, Crown 8vo. 1s.

BROWN—CAMBUSLANG : A SKETCH OF THE PLACE AND THE PEOPLE EARLIER THAN THE NINETEENTH CENTURY. By J. T. T. BROWN. With Two Etchings. Crown 8vo. 6d. Large paper copies with proofs of Etchings, 6s.

BROWN—THE LIFE OF A SCOTTISH PROBATIONER. Being the Memoir of THOMAS DAVIDSON, with his POEMS and LETTERS. By the REV. JAMES BROWN, D.D., of St. James' Church, Paisley. Second Edition. Crown 8vo. 7s. 6d.

"A charming little biography. His was one of those rare natures which fascinates all who come in contact with it."—*Spectator*.

"A worthy record of a man of rare genius—dead ere his prime. His poems are as beautiful as flowers or birds."—Dr. John Brown, Author of "Rab and his Friends."

"'This life of an unknown Scotch probationer is equal in interest to anything of the kind we have had since Carlyle's 'Life of Sterling' was written. Thomas Davidson, as a poet, as a humourist, as a simple, loving, honest, reticent, valiant soul, demands adequate recognition at the hands of the critic—a career kind and unostentatious, glorified, however, in its uneventful homeliness by a rare vein of poetry and a rich vein of humour."—*Blackwood's Magazine*.

"It is an unspeakable pleasure to a reviewer weary of wading through piles of commonplace to come unexpectedly on a prize such as this."—*Nonconformist*.

"A very fresh and interesting little book."—*Saturday Review*.

BUCHANAN—CAMP LIFE IN THE CRIMEA AS SEEN BY A CIVILIAN. A Personal Narrative by GEORGE BUCHANAN, M.A., M.D., Professor of Clinical Surgery in the University of Glasgow. Crown 8vo. 7s. 6d.

CAIRD, Principal—UNIVERSITY SERMONS AND LECTURES. By the Very REV. JOHN CAIRD, D.D., Principal and Vice-Chancellor of the University of Glasgow. 8vo. 1s. each.

1. WHAT IS RELIGION?

2. CHRISTIAN MANLINESS.

3. IN MEMORIAM. A Sermon on the Death of the Very Rev. Principal THOMAS BARCLAY, D.D.

4. THE UNIVERSAL RELIGION. A Lecture delivered in Westminster Abbey, on the day of Intercession for Missions.

5. THE UNITY OF THE SCIENCES. A Lecture.

6. THE PROGRESSIVENESS OF THE SCIENCES. A Lecture.

CAIRD, Principal—AN INTRODUCTION TO THE PHILOSOPHY OF RELIGION. By the VERY REVEREND JOHN CAIRD, D.D., Principal and Vice-Chancellor of the University of Glasgow, and one of Her Majesty's Chaplains for Scotland. Third Thousand. Demy 8vo. 10s. 6d.

" A book rich in the results of speculative study, broad in its intellectual grasp, and happy in its original suggestiveness. To Dr. Caird we are indebted for a subtle and masterly presentation of Hegel's philosophy in its solution of the problem of religion. In addition to the literary skill which places his propositions in their brightest light, and an earnestness of purpose which at times rises into genuine eloquence, he possesses two qualifications which specially fit him for his work : a spirit of reverence which places him in sympathy with mystical and intentional minds; and an intellectual vigour which enables him to stand side by side with the ablest thinkers, to view the utmost border of their extended range of vision, and, while he treats them with chivalrous fairness, to grapple with their arguments."—*Edinburgh Review.*

"It is the business of the reviewer to give some notion of the book which he reviews, either by a condensation of its contents or by collecting the cream in the shape of short selected passages ; but this cannot be done with a book like the one before us, of which the argument does not admit of condensation, and which is all cream.........The most valuable book of its kind that has appeared."—Mr. T. H. Green in *The Academy.*

" It is remarkable also for its marvellous power of exposition and graceful subtlety of thought. Hegelianism has never appeared so attractive as it appears in the clear and fluent pages of Principal Caird."—*Spectator.*

" Probably our British theological literature contains no nobler or more suggestive volume."—*Mind.*

CAIRD, Professor E.—A CRITICAL ACCOUNT OF THE PHILOSOPHY OF KANT : with an Historical Introduction. By EDWARD CAIRD, M.A., LL.D., Professor of Moral Philosophy in the University of Glasgow, and late Fellow and Tutor of Merton College, Oxford. 8vo.

[*New Edition in Preparation.*

CAMERON—LIGHT, SHADE, AND TOIL : POEMS. By a Working Man (WILLIAM C. CAMERON). Extra Fcap. 8vo. 6s.

CHURCH OF SCOTLAND—THE SCHEMES OF THE CHURCH. By a PARISH MINISTER. 25th Thousand. Crown 8vo. 2d.

CLELAND—Evolution, Expression, and Sensation. By John Cleland, M.D., D.Sc., F.R.S., Professor of Anatomy in the University of Glasgow. Crown 8vo. 5s.

" We recommend the essays of Professor Cleland in the warmest manner to all our readers.."—*Dublin Medical Journal.*

" Dr. Cleland's standing as a physiologist prepares us to find him discussing the matter with justice and calmness. He admits the services of Darwin to natural history, but points out some difficulties in the way of his famous Theory."—*British Medical Journal.*

" The reader can scarcely fail to be impressed with the marked originality of the work."—*Scotsman.*

CLELAND—The Relation of Brain to Mind. Cr. 8vo. 1s.

DEAS—History of the Clyde to the Present Time. With Maps and Diagrams. By James Deas, M. Inst. C.E., Engineer of the Clyde Navigation. 8vo. 10s. 6d.

DERBY, Earl of—Inaugural Address on his Installation as Lord Rector of the University of Glasgow. 8vo. 1s.

DICKSON—St. Paul's Use of the Terms Flesh and Spirit. Being the Baird Lecture for 1883. By William P. Dickson, D.D., Professor of Divinity in the University of Glasgow. Crown 8vo. 8s. 6d.

" This volume will take a permanent place in our theological literature as a full, able, and satisfactory treatise, by a ripe scholar and an accomplished theologian."—*N. B. Daily Mail.*

" This book is of interest to every one who wishes to read his New Testament intelligently and to follow the Apostle's meaning."—*Dundee Advertiser.*

" An able, thorough exposition."—*Scotsman.*

" Prof. Dickson has devoted much patience and conscientious labour to the mastery of all theories that have been presented down to the most recent, and has treated them with remarkable adroitness and impartiality. The work is essentially one for scholars."—*Daily Review.*

" Prof. Dickson is the first to give to the subject the earnest and elaborate treatment which it deserves, and the consequence is the book will be an indispensable help to the students of the Pauline Scriptures."—*Aberdeen Free Press.*

EGGS 4D. A DOZEN, AND CHICKENS 4D. A POUND
ALL THE YEAR ROUND. Containing full and com-
plete information for successful and profitable keeping of
Poultry. Small 8vo. Twentieth Thousand. 1s.

"The most complete little treatise on the rearing of poultry that has ever
come under our notice."—*Ayr Advertiser.*

" The small volume which is to revolutionize the popular notion of poultry
keeping."—*Newcastle Daily Chronicle.*

" Ought to be in the hands of every one who desires to make profit out of
the poultry he rears."—*Hamilton Advertiser.*

"Discusses the subject explicitly and exhaustively."—*Edinburgh Daily
Review.*

EWING—MEMOIR OF JAMES EWING, ESQ., M.P., of Strath-
leven. By the REV. M. MACKAY, LL.D. Fcap. 4to. 21s.

FORSYTH—A GRADUATED COURSE OF INSTRUCTION IN
LINEAR PERSPECTIVE. By DAVID FORSYTH, M.A., Lec-
turer in the Church of Scotland Training College, Glasgow.
In Royal 8vo. 2s.

"We are bound to say that this latest book is one of the best. In fact,
we know none that surpasses it. . . . The arrangement could hardly
be improved."—*Athenæum.*

" We gladly welcome this new work as a sound and useful guide both for
teacher and pupil."—*School Guardian.*

" Any youth of average intelligence with such a work in his hands ought
to feel little difficulty in mastering the principles of perspective, or getting
his certificate at South Kensington."—*Schoolmaster.*

" The book is convenient in form and size, and its ' get-up ' is excellent."
—*Educational Times.*

" This book is a model of clear and perspicuous teaching. Teachers will
find it an invaluable aid, and no student who has mastered it need fear to
face the Science and Art Department."—*Educational News.*

FORSYTH—TEST PAPERS IN PERSPECTIVE. A Series of
Papers for Testing the Progress of Pupils and for preparing
them for the Second Grade Examination of the Science and
Art Department. 24 different papers. Full Government
size. 1s. 6d. per set.

" The test papers are admirably adapted to familarize students with
examination work."—*Educational News.*

"Can hardly fail to be acceptable to teachers."—*Athenæum.*

FREELAND — A BIRTH SONG AND OTHER POEMS. By
WILLIAM FREELAND. Extra Foolscap 8vo. 6s.

" Always happy, tender, and pleasant."—*Dundee Advertiser.*
" Contains verses the world will not willingly let die."—*The Echo.*

GAIRDNER—MEDICAL EDUCATION, CHARACTER, AND CON-
DUCT. By W. T. GAIRDNER, M.D., Professor of Practice
of Medicine in the University of Glasgow, Physician in
Ordinary to the Queen. Crown 8vo. 1s.

GEMMEL—THE TIBERIAD ; or, The Art of Hebrew Accen-
tuation. By JOHN GEMMEL, D.D. Extra fcap. 8vo. 3s.

GLASGOW ARCHÆOLOGICAL SOCIETY'S TRANS-
ACTIONS. Second Series, 8vo. Part I., 5s. Part II., 5s.
Part III., 5s.

A few complete sets of the Transactions, in eight parts, demy
8vo, are now on sale, price £2 per set. Two of the parts which had
been long out of print have been reprinted in order to complete a limited
number of sets.

GLASGOW UNIVERSITY CALENDAR FOR THE YEAR
1884-85. *Published annually.* Crown 8vo., Cloth. 2s. 6d.

GLASGOW UNIVERSITY LOCAL EXAMINATIONS.
Scheme of Examinations for 1885, and Report for 1884.
*Published annually.* Crown 8vo. 6d.

GLASGOW—THE OLD COUNTRY HOUSES OF THE OLD
GLASGOW GENTRY. Illustrated by permanent Photographs.
Royal 4to. Half Red Morocco, gilt top. Second Edition.
*Very scarce.* £10, 10s.

This is a history of one hundred of the old houses in and around
Glasgow, and of the families who owned and lived in them. To the
local antiquary it is especially interesting as a memorial of the old burgher
aristocracy, of their character and habits, and of the city in which they
lived ; while to the descendants of the " old gentry " it is interesting as
containing the history of their forefathers and the rise of their families.

GLASGOW—MEMORABILIA OF THE CITY OF GLASGOW.
1568-1750. Fcap. 4to. Half Morocco. *Very scarce.* 63s.

GRANT—CATALOGUE OF 6415 STARS FOR THE EPOCH 1870, deduced from Observations made at the Glasgow University Observatory 1860-1881. By ROBERT GRANT, M.A., F.R.S., F.R.A.S., Professor of Astronomy in the University of Glasgow. 4to. *[Immediately.*

This volume has been printed at the expense of Her Majesty's Government as advised by the Council of the Royal Society.

GRANT—THE LORD'S SUPPER EXPLAINED. By the REV. WILLIAM GRANT, Ayr. Ninth Edition. 16mo. 4d.

GRANT—CHRISTIAN BAPTISM EXPLAINED. 16mo. 1s. 6d.

GRAY, David—THE POETICAL WORKS OF DAVID GRAY. New and enlarged Edition, extra Fcap. 8vo. 6s.

" Gems of poetry, exquisitely set."—*Glasgow News.*

HAMILTON, Janet—POEMS, ESSAYS, AND SKETCHES. By JANET HAMILTON. *[New Edition Immediately.*

"It is a book containing the Memoirs, Poems, and other Compositions of, to my mind, the most remarkable old woman I have ever heard of. . . . Certainly if some of her poems were placed among the poems of Burns in a volume of his, no one would for a moment doubt that they were the productions of the greatest of all the Scottish Poets. Hers, I think, is an amazing story. I confess it has surprised me beyond anything I have read for a long time."—The Right Hon. JOHN BRIGHT, M.P.

" One of the most remarkable books that has fallen into our hands for a long time past. It is a book that ennobles life."—*Athenæum.*

" The name of Janet Hamilton is one of the most remarkable in the history of Scottish poesy."—*Glasgow Herald.*

HEDDERWICK, James, LL.D.—THE VILLA BY THE SEA, AND OTHER POEMS. Extra Fcap. 8vo. 7s.

JEBB—THE ANABASIS OF XENOPHON.—Books III. and IV., with the Modern Greek Version of Constantine Bardalachos, and with an Introduction by R. C. JEBB, M.A., Professor of Greek in the University of Glasgow.

*[New Edition in Preparation.*

**LECKIE**—Sermons by Joseph Leckie, D.D., Ibrox, Glasgow. Crown 8vo. Second Thousand. 6s.

"This is a very remarkable volume. We have seldom read sermons so fresh and suggestive, and, although they were spoken sermons, so perfect in their literary form."—*Edinburgh Daily Review.*

"To those who want a volume of sound yet vigorous sermons, which will set their own minds thinking, we unhesitatingly say, get this without delay."—*Leeds Mercury.*

"Few congregations have the privilege of listening to such productions as these. Before we had read through a page it was evident that we were in the grasp of a mind of singular power and originality. There is nothing hackneyed, commonplace or tedious from beginning to end of the book."—*Christian World.*

**LEISHMAN**—A System of Midwifery, Including the Diseases of Pregnancy and the Puerperal State. By William Leishman, M.D., Regius Professor of Midwifery in the University of Glasgow. Demy 8vo. 880 pp., with 210 Engravings. Third Edition, revised. 21s.

"It is the best English work on the subject."—*Lancet.*

"We should counsel the student by all means to procure Dr. Leishman's work."—*London Medical Record.*

**LEITCH**—Practical Educationists and their Systems of Teaching. By James Leitch, late Principal of the Church of Scotland Normal School, Glasgow. Crown 8vo. 6s.

"This capital book presents us, in a compact and well-digested form, with all that is of most value in the really practical methods of the greatest educationists."—*School Board Chronicle.*

"Amid so much talking and writing about theory, Mr. Leitch's book comes as a happy relief, inasmuch as it deals with practical workers in hitherto rather neglected fields."—*Saturday Review.*

**MACEWEN**—Sermons. By Alexander MacEwen, M.A., D.D. With a Memoir by his Son. Crown 8vo. 6s.

**MACGEORGE**—Papers on the Principles and Real Position of the Free Church. By Andrew MacGeorge. 8vo. 6s.

M'KENDRICK—OUTLINES OF PHYSIOLOGY, IN ITS RELA-
TIONS TO MAN. By J. GRAY M'KENDRICK, M.D., F.R.S.,
Professor of Physiology in the University of Glasgow.
Crown 8vo. 750 pages, and 250 Engravings. 12s. 6d.

"We have much pleasure in confidently recommending this work to
students of medicine and others, as being the one of all others of recent
date best suited for their requirements."—*British Medical Journal.*
"An admirable book on physiology."—*British Quarterly Review.*
"The style is clear, and the illustrations numerous."—*Practitioner.*

M'KINLAY, J. Murray—Poems. Extra fcap. 8vo. 3s. 6d.

MACMILLAN—OUR LORD'S THREE RAISINGS FROM THE
DEAD. By the REV. HUGH MACMILLAN, LL.D., F.R.S.E.,
Author of "Bible Teachings in Nature." Crown 8vo. 6s.

"A spirit of earnest piety pervades the book ; its language is simple and
unaffected, and it abounds in apt and felicitous illustrations."—*Scotsman.*

MOODS—A POEM. Extra fcap. 8vo. 6s. 6d.

"This is a remarkable book. It is full of deep thought, of true insight
into nature, and of nimble fancies."—*Court Journal.*

MORTON—THE TREATMENT OF SPINA BIFIDA BY A NEW
METHOD. By JAMES MORTON, M.D., Professor of Materia
Medica, Anderson's College. Crown 8vo. 5s.

MUIR, James, C.A.—MONEY. A Lecture. 8vo. 1s.

MUIRHEAD—M. TULLIUS CICERO. A Chapter Introductory
to the Study of his Life and Works. By J. H. MUIRHEAD,
B.A., Oxon. Crown 8vo. 1s. 6d.

MÜLLER—OUTLINES OF HEBREW SYNTAX. By DR. AUGUST
MÜLLER, Professor of Oriental Languages in the University
of Könisberg. Translated and Edited by James Robertson,
M.A., D.D., Professor of Oriental Languages in the Uni-
versity of Glasgow. Demy 8vo. Second Edition. 6s.

"It may be recommended as an able and thoroughly trustworthy intro-
duction to Hebrew syntax."—Professor S. R. Driver in *The Academy.*
"The work supplies a real want for English students. The translation
is excellent."—*Bibliotheca Sacra.*

MURRAY—OLD CARDROSS, a Lecture. By DAVID MURRAY, M.A., F.S.A. Crown 8vo, 1s. 6d. Large paper copies, on Dutch Paper, 6s.

NEWTON—SIR ISAAC NEWTON'S PRINCIPIA. Edited by SIR WILLIAM THOMSON, D.C.L., LL.D., F.R.S., Professor of Natural Philosophy in the University of Glasgow, and HUGH BLACKBURN, M.A. Crown 4to. 31s. 6d.

NICHOL—TABLES OF EUROPEAN HISTORY, LITERATURE AND ART, FROM A.D. 200 TO 1882, and of American History, Literature and Art. By JOHN NICHOL, M.A., Balliol, Oxon., LL.D., Professor of English Language and Literature in the University of Glasgow. Third Edition, revised and greatly enlarged. Royal 8vo. Printed in Five Colours. 7s. 6d.

"The Tables are clear, and form an admirable companion to the student of history, or indeed to any one who desires to revise his recollection of facts."—*Times*.

"In a word, the great leading facts of European history for nearly seventeen hundred years are here compressed with wonderful clearness into a single slim volume. The book is a triumph of systematization; it embodies the result of great research, and will be found an admirable guide to the student, as well as useful for purposes of rapid reference."—*Scotsman*.

"About as convenient a book of reference as could be found."—*Spectator*.

"To the devotees of literature and history Prof. Nichol's Tables will be simply invaluable."—*Leeds Mercury*.

"These Tables, set out as they are with all the advantages of clear arrangement, and of excellent typography, are likely to be most useful."—*Pall Mall Gazette*.

"We commend these Tables most cordially to the attention of teachers."—*Schoolmaster*.

"A great boon to students." –*Dundee Advertiser*.

NICHOL—TABLES OF ANCIENT LITERATURE AND HISTORY, FROM B.C. 1500 TO A.D. 200. 4to, Cloth. 4s. 6d.

"They constitute a most successful attempt to give interest to the chronology of literature, by setting before the eye the relation between the literature and the practical life of mankind."—*Observer*.

**NICHOL**—The Death of Themistocles, and other Poems. Extra fcap. 8vo. 7s. 6d.

"Dignified, careful, conscientious work throughout."—*Saturday Review*.

"A hymn more solemnly beautiful than 'Donna Vera' was never chanted to Pallas herself by the most inspired of her ancient votaries."—*Glasgow Herald*.

"Professor Nichol is a master of the English epic metre."—*Scotsman*.

**OLRIG GRANGE.** *See* Smith.

**PORTER, S. T.**—Christian Prophecy. Post 8vo. 7s. 6d.

**PULSFORD** -Sermons Preached in Trinity Church, Glasgow. By the Rev. William Pulsford, D.D. Crown 8vo. Cloth, Red Edges. Cheap Edition. 4s. 6d.

"The sermons have much of the brilliancy of thought and style by which Robertson fascinated his Brighton hearers."—*Daily Review*.

"He is a preacher, because he has been first a thinker."—*Spectator*.

**RANKINE**—Songs and Fables. By W. J. Macquorn Rankine, late Professor of Engineering in the University of Glasgow. With Portrait, and with Ten Illustrations by J. B. Second Edition. Extra fcap. 8vo. 6s.

**ROSS**—Scottish History and Literature to the Period of the Reformation. By the late John Ross, LL.D., Edinburgh. Edited, with a Memoir, by James Brown, D.D., author of "The Life of a Scottish Probationer." 8vo. 14s.

"Dr. Ross was deeply versed in old Scottish literature; his patriotic enthusiasm is intense, but duly controlled in expression by a sufficient sense of humour. His book is not a dry compendium of facts, but a vivid account of the national life of Scotland, viewed now from the political, and now from the literary point of view."—*Times*.

"A work of quite exceptional literary and historical value. Its peculiar character, as well as its special value, lies in its skilful combination of the early history of Scotland, with an adequate and thoroughly well-informed description of the development of the national thought in the national literature."—*Scotsman*.

"There is no trace in this volume of mental weariness or perfunctory cram. It is nothing short of masterly. The style is full, nervous, perspicuous, vitalized by an enthusiasm always kept on the safe side by humour and good sense. In the warmth of his patriotic and moral enthusiasm, in his thorough mastery of details, as well as in the glowing energy of his style, he reminds us of Mr. Green."—*Academy*.

ROSS, W. T.—POEMS.   New Edition.   Extra fcap. 8vo.   6s.

ROSS, W. T.—WAIFS.  Essays and Sketches.  Ex. fcap. 8vo. 5s.

SCHLOMKA. — A GERMAN GRAMMAR.   By CLEMENS SCHLOMKA, M.A., Ph.D.                          [*Immediately.*

## 𝔓𝔬𝔢𝔪𝔰 𝔟𝔶 𝔱𝔥𝔢 𝔄𝔲𝔱𝔥𝔬𝔯 𝔬𝔣 "𝔒𝔩𝔯𝔦𝔤 𝔊𝔯𝔞𝔫𝔤𝔢."

SMITH—KILDROSTAN : a Dramatic Poem.   By the Author of "Olrig Grange."  Ex. fcap. 8vo.  7s. 6d.        [*This Day.*

"'Kildrostan' has all the interest and excitement of a novel, combined with the charm of dignified verse, and enhanced by the stimulus of manly thought. . . . The poem is one of unquestionable power. Scattered all through the five acts there are gems of thought which are enhanced in literary value by their brilliant setting. Dr. Smith's power of passionate utterance reaches its highest point in the scene, in the third act, in which Tremain's intense declarations of love are received by Doris with scoffs and jeers. It is like the play of lightning on an iceberg, brilliant but harmless. —*Scotsman.*

"Since the death of Scott hardly any man has so nearly approached the Wizard of the North in the art of telling a story in graphic and musical verse. . . . On Doris Cattanach Mr. Smith has extended his full strength, and not even the worldly-wise mother in 'Olrig Grange' nor Hilda Dalguise, nor even Winifred Urquhart is so powerfully drawn. On Tremain, the æsthetic poet, equal care has been bestowed. The æsthetic school has never been so fully explained or exposed. The prophet of culture is not encountered by parody or by satire, but by what we may term psychological anatomy, and the effect is irresistible."—*Echo.*

"'Kildrostan' is one of the very finest dramatic poems of the day."— *Fifeshire Journal.*

SMITH—OLRIG GRANGE : a Poem in Six Books.   By WALTER C. SMITH. Third Edition. Ex. fcap. 8vo. 6s. 6d.

"This remarkable poem will at once give its anonymous author a high place among contemporary English poets.—*Examiner.*

"The most sickening phase of our civilization has scarcely been exposed with a surer and quieter point, even by Thackeray himself, than in this advice of a fashionable and religious mother to her daughter."—*Pall Mall.*

"The story is told in powerful and suggestive verse."—*Spectator.*

"The pious self-pity of the worldly mother, and the despair of the worldly daughter are really brilliantly put. The story is worked out with quite uncommon power."--*Academy.*

SMITH—HILDA ; AMONG THE BROKEN GODS : a Poem. By the Author of " Olrig Grange." Third Edition. Extra fcap. 8vo. 7s. 6d.

" That it is characterized by vigorous thinking, delicate fancy, and happy terms of expression, is admitted on all hands."—*Times.*

" A poem of remarkable power."—*British Quarterly Review.*

" It is to ' Hilda,' however, that we must turn for the most tragic conception of actual life that has hitherto been fashioned into verse. No modern poet, it may safely be said, has plunged so deeply into the innermost heart of living men and women, and none has used such remarkable materials for his drama."—*Scottish Review.*

SMITH—NORTH COUNTRY FOLK. Poems by Author of " Olrig Grange." Ex. fcap. 8vo. 7s. 6d.

" These poems are really dramatic, genuinely pathetic, and will bear reading over and over again."—*Westminster Review.*

" The follies and pettiness of suburban life provoke Dr. Smith's scorn. The race for wealth, the desire for position, and other kindred themes, are treated in a straightforward, outspoken fashion."—*Dundee Advertiser.*

" ' Wee Curly Pow ' is full of exquisite pathos and tenderness, and ' Dick Dalgleish ' is rich in genuine humour. We recommend all who are fond of genuine poetry to get Dr. Smith's poems at once. The book is full of music."—*Sheffield Independent.*

" For rich variety alike in substance and form, for scathing exposure of all that is mean and base, and for the effective presentation of the loftiest ideals, for mingled humour and pathos, we do not know a volume in the whole range of Scottish verse that can be said to surpass ' North Country Folk '."—*Christian Leader.*

SMITH—BORLAND HALL : a Poem. By the Author of " Olrig Grange." [*Third Edition in preparation.*

SMITH—RABAN ; OR, LIFE SPLINTERS : a Poem. By the Author of " Olrig Grange." [*Second Edition in preparation.*

SMITH—BISHOP'S WALK ; and Other Poems. Extra fcap. 8vo. 2s. 6d.

SPREULL—WRITINGS OF JOHN SPREULL (commonly called Bass John) 1646-1722. Edited by J. W. BURNS, of Kilmahew. Extra fcap. 4to. With Facsimiles and Portrait. 12s. 6d.

STANLEY, Dean—THE BURNING BUSH. A Sermon. 8vo. 1s.

STEWART—THE PLAN OF ST. LUKE'S GOSPEL.  By WILLIAM STEWART, M.A., D.D., Professor of Biblical Criticism in the University of Glasgow.  8vo.  3s. 6d.

STODDART—VILLAGE LIFE: A Poem.  By JAMES H. STODDART, Editor of the *Glasgow Herald.* Extra fcap. 8vo. 6s. 6d.

"A remarkable volume of poetry, which will be read by all who have any keen interest in the progress of English literature."—*Standard.*

STORY—CREED AND CONDUCT : Sermons preached in Rosneath Church.  By ROBERT HERBERT STORY, D.D., Minister of the Parish.  Crown 8vo.  Cheap Edition.  3s. 6d.

"In all respects this volume is worthy to be placed alongside of those of Caird and Guthrie, Tulloch and Service."—*Glasgow Herald.*
"These are excellent sermons.  They are sensible, manly, scholarly, and religious."—*Edinburgh Courant.*
"Characterized throughout by profound earnestness and spirituality, and written in a style at once graceful, clear, and nervous."—*Scotsman.*
"We heartily commend the book to our readers."—*Dundee Advertiser.*

VEITCH—THE HISTORY AND POETRY OF THE SCOTTISH BORDER, THEIR MAIN FEATURES AND RELATIONS.  By JOHN VEITCH, LL.D., Professor of Logic and Rhetoric in the University of Glasgow.  Crown 8vo.  10s. 6d.

"This is a genuine book.  We heartily recommend it."—*Contemporary Review.*
"We feel as if we were hearing the stories, or listening to the snatches of song among the breezes of the mountains or the moorland, under the sun-broken mists of the wild glens, or the wooded banks of the Yarrow or the Tweed."—*Times.*
"The fullest, most thorough, and most deeply critical work on Border history and poetry that we have."—*British Quarterly Review.*

VEITCH—HILLSIDE RHYMES.  Extra fcap. 8vo.  5s.

VEITCH—THE TWEED, AND OTHER POEMS.  Extra fcap. 8vo. 6s. 6d.

VEITCH—LUCRETIUS AND THE ATOMIC THEORY.  Crown 8vo.  3s. 6d.

WADDELL—OSSIAN AND THE CLYDE ; or, Ossian Historical and Authentic. By P. HATELY WADDELL, LL.D. 4to. 12s. 6d.

WATSON—KANT AND HIS ENGLISH CRITICS, a Comparison of Critical and Empirical Philosophy. By JOHN WATSON, M.A., LL.D., Professor of Moral Philosophy in Queen's University, Kingston, Canada. 8vo. 12s. 6d.

"Decidedly the best exposition of Kant which we have seen in English. We cannot too strongly commend it."—*Saturday Review.*

" C'est l'oeuvre d'un penseur et d'un maître. . . . Nous avons lu le livre de M. Watson avec un vif intérêt et une grande sympathie."—*Revue Philosophique.*

"This book is written with clearness and precision, and the author is thoroughly impregnated with the doctrine which he expounds, and makes it as plain as it can be made without becoming other than it is."—Professor T. H. GREEN, in the *Academy.*

" All students of Kant will recognize his thorough mastery of the system he expounds."—*Scotsman.*

---

# *New Books and New Editions*
# *In Preparation.*

PROFESSOR CAIRD—THE PHILOSOPHY OF KANT. By EDWARD CAIRD, M.A., LL.D., late Fellow and Tutor of Merton College, Oxford ; Professor of Moral Philosophy in the University of Glasgow. Demy 8vo.

MONS. GORECKI—A FRENCH GRAMMAR. By A. L. GORECKI, Lecturer in the Church of Scotland Training College, Glasgow.

### *New Books in Preparation.—Continued.*

*PROFESSOR GRANT*—CATALOGUE OF 6415 STARS for the Epoch 1870, deduced from Observations made at the Glasgow University Observatory.   By ROBERT GRANT, M.A., F.R.S., F.R.A.S., Director of the Observatory, and Professor of Astronomy in the University of Glasgow. Demy 4to, 800 pp.

*JANET HAMILTON*—POEMS, ESSAYS, AND SKETCHES. Crown 8vo.                              [*New Edition immediately.*

*PROFESSOR JEBB*—THE ANABASIS OF XENOPHON.—Books III. and IV., with the Modern Greek Version of Constantine Bardalachos, and with an Introduction by R. C. JEBB, M.A. Professor of Greek in the University of Glasgow.

[*New Edition in preparation.*

*PROFESSOR JEBB*—A NEW SELECTION OF GREEK EXTRACTS.   By R. C. JEBB, M.A., Professor of Greek in the University of Glasgow.

*PROFESSOR NICHOL*—ESSAYS ON ENGLISH LITERATURE. By JOHN NICHOL, M.A. Balliol, Oxon, LL.D., Professor of English Language and Literature in the University of Glasgow.

### By the Author of "Olrig Grange."

*BORLAND HALL:* a Poem.   By WALTER C. SMITH, M.A., Author of " Olrig Grange."   [*Third Edition in preparation.*

*RABAN:* a Poem.   By the Author of " Olrig Grange."

[*Second Edition in preparation.*

*MR. ROSS*—THE FINE ARTS AND OTHER ESSAYS.

*DR. SCHLOMKA*—A GERMAN GRAMMAR.   By CLEMENS SCHLOMKA, M.A., Ph.D., German Master in the Glasgow High School.

www.ingramcontent.com/pod-product-compliance
Lightning Source LLC
Chambersburg PA
CBHW020923120726
47905CB00008B/2353